BREAKFAST COOKBOOK

Quick & Easy Paleo Breakfast Recipes for the Whole Family

(Delicious and Quick Breakfast Recipes to Fight Inflammation)

Mary Smith

Published by Alex Howard

© **Mary Smith**

All Rights Reserved

Breakfast Cookbook: Quick & Easy Paleo Breakfast Recipes for the Whole Family (Delicious and Quick Breakfast Recipes to Fight Inflammation)

ISBN 978-1-990169-57-1

All rights reserved. No part of this guide may be reproduced in any form without permission in writing from the publisher except in the case of brief quotations embodied in critical articles or reviews.

Legal & Disclaimer

The information contained in this book is not designed to replace or take the place of any form of medicine or professional medical advice. The information in this book has been provided for educational and entertainment purposes only.

The information contained in this book has been compiled from sources deemed reliable, and it is accurate to the best of the Author's knowledge; however, the Author cannot guarantee its accuracy and validity and cannot be held liable for any errors or omissions. Changes are periodically made to this book. You must consult your doctor or get professional medical advice before using any of the suggested remedies, techniques, or information in this book.

Table of contents

Part 1 1

Introduction 2

Low Carb Buttermilk Pancakes 3

Flax Pancake 4

Spinach Quiche 5

Southwest Breakfast Casserole 6

Cheesy Bacon Frittata 7

Low Carb Crepes 8

Onion And Green Pepper Quiche 9

Zucchini Breakfast Muffins 10

Swiss Cheese And Sausage Quiche 12

Cream Cheese Muffins 13

Mushroom And Spinach Quiche 14

Bacon Breakfast Skillet (Keto Friendly) 15

Orange Muffins 16

Easy Protein Pancakes 18

Low Carb Breakfast Bites 19

Caramelized Onions And Pepper Quiche 20

Sausage And Zucchini Quiche 21

Turkey Breakfast Balls 22

Mexican Breakfast Casserole 23

Basil Quiche 24

Sausage And Mushroom Quiche 25

Ham And Swiss Breakfast Skillet 26

Creamy Sausage Breakfast Casserole (Keto Friendly) 27

Turkey Breakfast Muffins 28
Pancake Breakfast Sandwiches (Keto Friendly) 29
Pepper Jack Quiche 30
Crepes 31
Ever Waffles 32
Microwave Poached Eggs 33
Basic Batter Waffles 34
Oatmeal Cottage Cheese Pancakes 35
Wheat Pancakes 36
Sausage Gravy 37
Roasted Bacon 38
Strawberry Smoothie 39
Cinnamon Muffins 40
Zucchini Bread 41
Chocolate Chip Pancakes 42
Perfect Soft Boiled Eggs 43
Leftover Mashed Potato Pancakes 44
Favorite Oatmeal Pancakes 45
Gluten Waffles 46
Peach Muffins 47
Fluffy Pancakes 48
Strawberry And Banana Smoothie 49
Spinach Banana Smoothie 50
Keto Pancakes 51
Keto Pancakes With Almond Flour 52
Pancakes With Coconut Flour 53
Keto Chocolate Muffins 54

Keto Pancakes With Berries	54
Keto Cauliflower Hash Browns	56
Keto Banana Waffles	57
Keto Coconut Pancakes	58
Pancakes With Cream-Cheese	59
Keto Cinnamon Pancakes	60
Keto Croque Monsieur	61
Keto French Pancakes	62
Keto Blueberry Pancakes	63
Whipped Cream And Berries	64
Keto Buttercream	65
Keto Hazelnut Spread	66
Keto Scrambled Eggs	67
Keto Scrambled Eggs With Cheese	68
Keto Scrambled Eggs With Butter	69
Keto Cinnnamon Roll Muffins	70
Blueberry Coconut Flour Muffins	72
Keto Zucchini Muffins	72
Keto Muffins With Ham	75
Cinnamon Walnut Muffins	77
Peanut Butter Muffins	79
Egg Muffins	79
Banana Muffins	81
Cake Muffins	81
Prosciutto Egg Muffins	83
Cinnamon Donut Muffins	85
10 Minute Muffins	85

Keto Breakfast Burrito 87

Keto Coconut Waffles.. 88

Coconut Crepes 89

Almond Butter Crepes 90

Rooibos Tea Latte 91

Keto Bagels.. 92

Keto Tacos With Bacon 92

Keto Breakfast Wrap 93

Soft Boiled Eggs With Butter 95

1. Ultimate Camping Breakfast Sandwich 96

2. Peach Chia Overnight Oats 97

3. Kielbasa Pepper Onion And Hash...................................... 98

4. Cheesy Bacon And Eggs Hash... 100

5. Vegan Banana Coconut French Toast............................. 102

6. Easy Camping Parfaits 104

7. Bacon Hashbrown Breakfast Sandwich 105

8. Campfire French Toast.. 107

9. Breakfast Burrito À La Camping....................................... 109

10. Hot Ham And Swiss Croissants...................................... 111

11. Egg And Sausage Breakfast Taquitos........................... 112

12. Egg In A Basket... 114

13. Fried Potatoes... 115

14. Campfire Bacon 117

15. Camping Hash Browns... 118

16. Campfire Apple Crisp Breakfast.................................... 119

17. Simple Yogurt And Nuts For Camping 121

18. Campfire Breakfast Burger... 122

19. Hot Ham And Pineapple Campfire Sandwiches 124

20. Campfire Skillet Oreo Cinnamon Buns 126

21. Mountain Man Breakfast Casserole 128

22. Campfire Beer Pancakes 130

23. Breakfast Tortillas 132

24. Cinnamon Blueberry Bread 134

25. Camping Quesadillas 136

26. Blueberry Orange Muffins 138

27. Campfire Eclairs 139

28. Toasted Angel Food Cake With Berries 140

29. Indian Spiced Baked Potato And Egg Foil Packets 141

30. Lumberjack Breakfast 143

Part 2 145

Introduction 146

Breakfast And Health Benefits 147

Cheese Health Benefits 151

Butter In Keto Diet And Health Benefits 155

Nutritional Value Of Eggs In Keto Diet 158

RECIPES 161

Almond Flour Pancakes 161

Blackberry Cobbler 163

Breakfast Brownie Muffins 165

Mushroom Ricotta Galette 167

Blueberry Pancakes 169

Chocolate Waffles 171

Creamy Keto Oatmeal 173

Rosemary Keto Bagels 175

Mexican Breakfast Hash 177
Cauliflower Hash Browns 179
Berries Cream Cake 180
Classic French Omelet 181
Cheesy Waffles 183
Rutabaga Avocado Fritters 185
French Toast Muffins 187
Conclusion 189

Part 1

Introduction

The low carb diet is one of the most proven and effective diets for losing weight. As you probably assumed, the low carb diet is based on consuming foods that are low in carbohydrates. It can be difficult to know exactly which foods are high in carbs however. Below are some useful tips for anyone on the low carb diet.

Here are some helpful low carb dieting tips:
- Include vegetables and lean meats (fish and chicken) in your diet. Most vegetables and meats contain low amounts of carbs, and can control your appetite.
- Avoid starchy foods like pasta, potatoes, and rice. These foods have high amounts of carbs!
- Stick to drinking water, most other drinks like juice may include sugars that you may not be aware of.

This low carb cookbook has a wide range of beginner friendly low carb recipes for you to enjoy. These recipes will help you avoid carbs, and they also taste great!

Low Carb Buttermilk Pancakes

Ingredients

1 cup almond flour

1/4 tsp baking powder

Dash salt

3 eggs

1/2 tsp vanilla

1 tsp granular Splenda

2 tbsp water, as needed

Directions

Mix all of the ingredients, except the water, in a medium bowl with a fork.

Add enough water until a pancake batter consistency. Heat some oil in a nonstick skillet over medium heat until water on the pan sizzles.

Add around 1/4 cup batter per pancake into the skillet and cook on both sides until golden brown.

Flip pancakes when air bubbles appear.

Makes 4 pancakes
Nutrition: 179 Calories; 14g Fat; 9g Protein;; 2.5g Net Carbs per pancake

Flax Pancake

Ingredients

3 tbsp golden flax meal

1 tsp granular Splenda or equivalent liquid Splenda

1/4 tsp baking powder

1 dash salt

1 large egg

1 tbsp butter, melted

1 tbsp water

Directions

In a small bowl, combine the dry ingredients. Add the wet ingredients and mix well with a fork.

Pour into a greased 8-9" glass pie plate. Spread batter to cover the bottom of the pan. Microwave on HIGH 1 1/2-3 minutes, until cooked through but still soft.

Serve with sugar free syrup.

Makes 1 large pancake

Nutrition: 275 Calories; 24g Fat; 10g Protein;2g Net Carbs per pancake

Spinach Quiche

Ingredients

2 ounces onion, chopped

2 medium mushrooms, sliced, 1 ounce

1 tbsp butter

10 oz package frozen chopped spinach, thawed and drained very well

2/3 cup ham, diced, optional

5 eggs

12 oz cheddar cheese, shredded

1/8 tsp pepper

1/2 tsp salt

Directions

Sauté the onion and mushrooms in the butter until tender. Add the spinach and ham; stir and cook until heated and mixed well.

Put the cheese in a greased pie plate. Mix in the spinach mixture. Beat the eggs, salt and pepper.

Pour evenly over the spinach; mix well. Bake 350º for 25-35 minutes.

Nutrition: 350 Calories; 27g Fat; 23g Protein; 3g Net Carbs per 1/6 of recipe

Southwest Breakfast Casserole

Ingredients

10 eggs

1 cup cheese blend

2 jalapeno chicken sausages, diced

1 green bell pepper, diced

1 tsp cajun seasoning

1/4 tsp black pepper

Directions

Preheat oven to 375F. Use nonstick cooking spray or olive oil to grease a 8x8 glass baking dish.

Layer sausage, peppers, and cheese in the bottom of the dish. In a separate bowl, use a fork or whisk to combine egg yolks and whites with the cajun seasoning and pepper.

Be sure all yolks are combined. Pour eggs over layers in baking dish and use fork to stir, ensuring ingredients are equally mixed.

Bake in oven for 25-30 minutes, or until lightly browned on top. Allow to cool slightly before cutting.

May be stored in refrigerator in separate containers for easy reheating.

Nutrition: 217 Calories; 13g Fat; 19g Protein; 4g Net Carbs per 1/6 of recipe

Cheesy Bacon Frittata

Ingredients

6 eggs

1 cup heavy cream

1/2 tsp salt

1/4 tsp pepper

2 green onions, chopped

5 slices bacon, fried until crisp

4 oz cheddar cheese

Directions

Beat the eggs, cream and seasonings. Pour into a large greased pie plate. Top with the remaining ingredients and bake at 350º 30-35 minutes.

Let stand a few minutes before serving.

Nutrition: 320 Calories; 29g Fat; 13g Protein; 2g Net Carbs per 1/6 of recipe

Low Carb Crepes

Ingredients

2 eggs

2 egg yolks

Dash of salt

1 cup Carbalose flour

1/2 cup heavy cream

1/2 cup water

1 tablespoon butter, melted

Directions

In a medium mixing bowl, combine the eggs, yolks and salt. Gradually whisk in the flour alternately with the cream and water until smooth. Whisk in the butter.

Chill the batter at least 1 hour. Heat a 9 or 10-inch nonstick skillet on medium heat, spraying very lightly with cooking spray.

Lift the skillet off the heat and make each crepe by pouring in 2 tablespoons of the batter while tilting the pan in all directions to swirl the batter in a thin even layer.

Cook until the bottom of the crepe is browned; flip and brown the other side for a few seconds.

Nutrition: 108 Calories; 9g Fat; 5g Protein; 2g Net Carbs per crepe

Onion And Green Pepper Quiche

Ingredients

1 green pepper, cut in thin strips, 4 ounces

2 oz onion, slivered

1-2 tbsp butter

8 oz Monterey jack cheese, shredded

6 eggs

1 cup heavy cream

1/2 tsp salt

Dash pepper

Directions

Sauté the peppers and onion in butter until tender. Place the cheese in a greased large pie plate.

Top with the pepper mixture. Beat the eggs with the cream, salt and pepper. Pour evenly over the peppers.

Bake at 350F° 35 minutes, until a knife inserted in the center comes out clean. Let stand 10 minutes before cutting.

Nutrition: 393 Calories; 35g Fat; 17g Protein; 4g Net Carbs per 1/6 of recipe

Zucchini Breakfast Muffins

Makes 6 muffins

Ingredients

4 oz almond flour

1/2 cup golden flax meal

1 tsp baking powder

1/8 tsp salt

1 tsp cinnamon

3/4 cup granular Splenda or equivalent liquid Splenda

1/2 tsp blackstrap molasses

1 tsp vanilla

1/2 tsp caramel extract, optional

2 tbsp heavy cream

2 tbsp water

2 tbsp butter, softened

2 eggs

3/4 cup shredded zucchini, tightly packed

Directions

In a medium bowl, stir together the almond flour, flax meal, baking powder, salt, cinnamon and granular

Splenda, if using. If you're using liquid Splenda, mix it in a custard dish with the extract, cream and water.

Combine everything with the dry ingredients and stir with a wooden spoon until well blended.

Fill 6 paper-lined muffin cups with the batter, dividing it evenly among them.

Bake at 350F° 20-26 minutes, until the tops are golden brown. Remove from the pan and cool on a rack.

Serve warm or at room temperature.

Nutrition: 204 Calories; 17g Fat; 7g Protein; 6g Net Carbs per muffin

Swiss Cheese And Sausage Quiche

Ingredients

1/2 pound smoked sausage

6 ounces Swiss cheese, shredded

6 eggs

3/4 cup heavy cream

1/2 teaspoon salt

1 teaspoon chives, minced

Directions

Peel the skin off the smoked sausage and cut in half lengthwise. Cut each half into halfmoons. In a medium bowl, whisk the eggs.

Add the cream, salt and chives; whisk well. Arrange the cheese and sausage evenly in the bottom of a greased 9-10 inch glass pie plate.

Pour the egg mixture over the cheese. Bake at 350F°, 35-40 minutes, until a knife inserted in the center comes out clean.

Nutrition: 410 Calories; 35g Fat; 20g Protein; 4g Net Carbs per 1/6 of recipe

Cream Cheese Muffins

Makes 12 muffins

Ingredients

8 oz cream cheese, softened

3 eggs

2 oz almond flour

1 cup Carbalose flour

1 tsp baking powder

1/2 cup sugar free syrup, vanilla flavor

1 cup granular Splenda

1 tsp cinnamon

Directions

Beat the cream cheese with an electric mixer until smooth. Beat in the eggs. Add all of the remaining ingredients except the topping.

Fill 12 greased muffin cups. Bake at 350º 25-30 minutes. Mix the 2 teaspoons granular Splenda and 1/4 teaspoon cinnamon.

While the muffins are hot from the oven, brush with the melted butter and sprinkle with the Splenda-cinnamon mixture.

Nutrition: 155 Calories; 12g Fat; 7g Protein; 5g Net Carbs per muffin

Mushroom And Spinach Quiche

Ingredients

1 tbsp butter

8 oz fresh mushrooms, sliced

4 oz red onion, chopped fine, 1 medium

10 oz frozen spinach, thawed and drained

5 eggs

1/2 cup heavy cream

1/2 tsp salt

1/4 tsp pepper

8 oz sharp cheddar cheese, shredded

Directions

In a large skillet, sauté the mushrooms and onions in the butter until tender. Remove from the heat and stir in the spinach.

In a large bowl, whisk the eggs. Whisk in the cream, salt and pepper. Add the mushroom mixture and stir well.

Stir in the cheese. Pour everything into a greased 10-inch pie plate.

Bake at 350º 35-40 minutes or until set and lightly browned. Let stand 10 minutes before serving.

Nutrition: 174 Calories; 14g Fat; 8g Protein; 4g Net Carbs per 1/6 of recipe

Bacon Breakfast Skillet (Keto Friendly)

Ingredients

6 large eggs

1/2 package of bacon

2 tbsp of salted Butter

2 tsp of pepper

1/2 medium onion

1 cup cheddar cheese

Directions

Cook the bacon until crispy and dice the onion.

Place the pepper, butter, and onions into a skillet over medium heat and cook until the onions are lightly brown, stirring occasionally.

Scramble the eggs in a mixing bowl while waiting for your onions to brown.

Once the onions are lightly brown, pour in the eggs and cook until the eggs are done.

Add the cheese to the eggs, and mix until the cheese is melted. Crumble up the crisp bacon, and add it to the mix.

Nutrition: 751 Calories; 61g Fat; 43g Protein; 6.5g Net Carbs per 1/2 of recipe

Orange Muffins

Makes 6 muffins

Ingredients

4 oz almond flour

1/2 cup golden flax meal

1 tsp baking powder

1/8 tsp salt

1 oz pecans, chopped

1 cup granular Splenda

2 tbsp butter

1 tsp pure orange extract

1 tsp vanilla

2 tbsp heavy cream

2 tbsp water or orange juice

1 tbsp orange zest (1 small orange)

2 eggs

Directions

In a small bowl, stir together the almond flour, flax meal, baking powder, salt, nuts and granular Splenda, if using.

In a medium microwave-safe bowl, melt the butter in the microwave. Stir in the liquid Splenda, if using, the extracts, cream, water and orange zest.

Add the dry ingredients and the eggs to the butter mixture; stir with a wooden spoon until well blended.

Fill 6 paper-lined muffin cups with the batter, dividing it evenly among them.

Bake at 350F° 15-20 minutes, until the tops are golden brown.

Cool 5 minutes on a rack before removing from the pan. Serve warm or at room temperature.

Nutrition: 284 Calories; 24g Fat; 8g Protein; 7g Net Carbs per muffin

Easy Protein Pancakes

Ingredients

1 rounded scoop of any flavor whey protein powder

4 egg whites

1 tsp cinnamon

sugar free maple syrup (for topping)

Directions

Combine the protein powder, egg whites, and cinnamon and use a hand blender or whisk by hand to combine well.

Fry in Pam in a skillet on medium heat.

Top with sugar free maple syrup.

Nutrition: 243 Calories; 2g Fat; 44g Protein; 13g Net Carbs per pancake

Low Carb Breakfast Bites

Makes 6 bites

Ingredients

6 large eggs

1/2 cup crumbled cooked bacon, sausage or ham (your choice)

3/4 cup shredded cheese

1/2 cup diced onions, peppers or tomatoes (optional)

Directions

Place a teaspoon of meat into each cup of the muffin pan. Then add your choice of vegetables.

Beat eggs in a liquid measuring cup with a spout.

Pour egg mixture just a little over half way. Top with shredded cheese.

Bake in the oven at 350F for 10-12 minutes.

Let cool, wrap each in plastic wrap. Heat as needed refrigerate the rest.

Nutrition: 155 Calories; 10g Fat; 13g Protein; 1.5g Net Carbs per bite

Caramelized Onions And Pepper Quiche

Ingredients

1 tbsp butter

1 medium onion, slivered, 4 ounces

8 oz Swiss cheese, shredded

1 large or 2 small roasted red peppers, cut in strips

6 eggs

1/2 cup heavy cream

1/2 tsp salt

1/4 tsp pepper

Directions

Sauté the onion in butter until golden brown. Put the cheese, red peppers and onions in a large greased pie plate.

In a medium bowl, beat the eggs, cream, salt and pepper untl well blended. Pour the egg mixture over the cheese and mix everything well.

Bake at 350F° about 35 minutes or until a knife inserted into the center comes out clean. Let stand 10 minutes before cutting and serving.

Nutrition: 312 Calories; 25g Fat; 18g Protein; 4g Net Carbs per 1/6 of recipe

Sausage And Zucchini Quiche

Ingredients

7 oz zucchini, shredded, 1 medium or 2 cups

2 tbsp butter

1/2 pound Italian sausage, browned and drained

4 oz Swiss cheese, shredded

1 oz parmesan cheese, 1/4 cup

5 eggs

1 cup heavy cream

1/2 tsp salt

Dash pepper

Directions

Sauté the zucchini in butter 5 minutes. Place in the bottom of a greased 10-inch pie plate and pat dry with paper towel.

Top with the sausage and Swiss cheese. Beat the eggs, cream, parmesan and seasonings; pour over the sausage.

Bake at 450º 15 minutes. Turn down the heat to 350Fº and bake 15-20 minutes longer or until browned and a knife inserted in center comes out clean.

Check after 15 minutes because it will get quite brown. Let stand 10 minutes before serving.

Nutrition: 461 Calories; 41g Fat; 19g Protein; 3.5g Net Carbs per 1/6 of recipe

Turkey Breakfast Balls

Ingredients

2 lbs turkey sausage

1 lb ground turkey

3 eggs

2 tbsp dried onion flakes

1/2 lb shredded cheddar cheese

2 tbsp ground flaxseed

1/4 cup whey protein

Directions

Mix all ingredients together until thoroughly blended either by hand or with a hand mixer

Form into about 4 dozen 1-1.5 inch balls and place on a cookie sheet or broiler pan

Bake at 375F for 25 minutes

Once cool, store in individual ziploc bags.

Nutrition: 170 Calories; 8g Fat; 23g Protein; 1.5g Net Carbs per 1/12of recipe

Mexican Breakfast Casserole

Ingredients

12 ounces pork sausage

1/2 teaspoon garlic powder

1/2 teaspoon coriander

1 teaspoon cumin

1 teaspoon chili powder

1/4 teaspoon salt

1/4 teaspoon pepper

1 cup salsa

10 eggs

1 cup milk

1 cup Pepper Jack cheese or your choice of cheese

Optional toppings: sour cream. avocado, salsa, cilantro

Directions

In a large skillet over medium heat, cook the pork sausage until no longer pink. Add seasonings and salsa. Set aside to cool slightly.

In a another bowl whisk the eggs and milk. Add the pork to the eggs, then add the cheese and stir to combine.

Grease the bottom of the crock pot and pour in mixture. Cover and cook on high 2 1/2 hours or low 5 hours.

Serve with optional toppings.

Nutrition: 196 Calories; 8g Fat; 18g Protein; 5g Net Carbs per 1/10 of recipe

Basil Quiche

Ingredients

Olive oil

1 cup onion, chopped

1 clove garlic, minced

3 oz mozzarella cheese, shredded

4 oz Roma tomatoes, sliced thin

1/4 cup fresh basil, shredded fine

1/2 cup heavy cream

1/2 cup water

1/4 tsp pepper

1/2 tsp salt

6 eggs

Directions

Grease a 9-10" pie plate. Sauté the onions and garlic in oil until slightly browned. Spread in the bottom of quiche pan.

Top with the cheese. Arrange the tomato slices over the cheese. Top with the basil. Mix the cream, water, salt, pepper and eggs; whisk well.

Pour evenly over everything in the pan.

Bake at 350F° for 35 minutes until a knife inserted in center comes out clean. Let stand 10 minutes before cutting.

Nutrition: 221 Calories; 18g Fat; 10g Protein; 3g Net Carbs per 1/6 of recipe

Sausage And Mushroom Quiche

Ingredients

1 pound pork sausage

1/2 pound fresh mushrooms, sliced

1 small onion, chopped, 2 1/2 ounces

8 oz cheddar cheese, shredded

6 eggs

1/2 teaspoon salt

Dash pepper

1 cup heavy cream

Directions

Brown the sausage along with the mushrooms and onions; drain the fat. Put the sausage mixture in the bottom of a large pie plate.

Top with the cheese. Beat the eggs, salt and pepper, then beat in the cream. Slowly pour the egg mixture evenly over the sausage and cheese.

Bake at 350F for 35-45 minutes until a knife inserted in center comes out clean. Let stand about 10 minutes before cutting.

Nutrition: 619 Calories; 53g Fat; 33g Protein; 4g Net Carbs per 1/6 of recipe

Ham And Swiss Breakfast Skillet

Ingredients

1 cup mushrooms, sliced, 2 1/2 ounces

1 green onion, sliced

1 tablespoon butter

1 small zucchini, chopped fine, 4 ounces

3/4 cup ham, chopped fine, about 3 slices lunchmeat

6 eggs

Dash salt

Dash pepper

2 ounces Swiss cheese

Chives, for garnish

Directions

Sauté the mushrooms, green onion and zucchini in butter in a large skillet until tender. Season with salt and pepper. Stir in the ham and sauté until hot.

Beat the eggs just until blended; season with salt and pepper. Pour the eggs over the ingredients in the skillet.

Cook on low, without stirring, until set on the bottom and edges. Lift the edges to let the raw egg flow underneath.

Top with the cheese; broil 5 inches from the heat for 1-2 minutes to melt the cheese.

If you don't have an oven-proof skillet, carefully slide everything onto a large platter or quiche pan.

Microwave about 2-3 minutes until the cheese is melted. Sprinkle the top with chives.

Nutrition: 164 Calories; 11g Fat; 12g Protein; 2g Net Carbs per 1/6 of recipe

Creamy Sausage Breakfast Casserole (Keto Friendly)

Ingredients

1 lb ground sausage

4 ounces softened cream cheese

1/2 small onion, diced

2 jalapeno peppers, diced (or 1/2 green pepper)

6 well-beaten eggs (season with salt and pepper)

1 cup shredded cheese

Directions

Preheat oven to 350F degrees. Spray a 9 x 13 pan with non-stick cooking spray. Brown sausage and drain excess grease.

Press sausage into the bottom of pan. Break cream cheese into pieces and evenly distribute on top of sausage.

Sprinkle with onions and peppers. Pour eggs over the sausage mixture. Add shredded cheese to the top.

Bake for 25 minutes, let cool before cutting.

Nutrition: 378 Calories; 97g Fat; 23g Protein; 6g Net Carbs per 1/5 of recipe

Turkey Breakfast Muffins

Ingredients

1 pound ground turkey

1 stalk celery, minced

1/3 cup shallots or onion, minced

2 ounces cheddar cheese, shredded

2 eggs

1/4 cup heavy cream

1/4 teaspoon pepper

1/4 teaspoon chicken seasoning

Directions

Brown the turkey with the celery, onion and a little salt and pepper until the celery is tender; drain off any grease.

Beat the eggs, cream, pepper and chicken seasoning. Divide the turkey among 6 well-greased muffin cups.

The cups will be very full. Top with the cheese then very slowly pour the egg mixture evenly over each one.

Bake at 350F° 20-25 minutes, until set and lightly browned.

Nutrition: 261 Calories; 20g Fat; 18g Protein; 1g Net Carbs per muffin

Pancake Breakfast Sandwiches (Keto Friendly)

Ingredients

Pancake ingredients:

2.25 oz pork skins

3 tbsp almond flour

3 large eggs

3 tbsp heavy cream

3/4 tsp Vanilla extract

6 tbsp sugar free or low carb syrup

3 Sausage patties

Filling ingredients:

3 egg patties

3 Sausage patties

3 slices cheese

Directions

Grind pork skins in food processor. Pour into bowl and stir in remaining pancake ingredients.

Using a round metal form (if you have one), place in pan with 1 tbsp oil and pour batter in to fill. If you do not have one just pour in as a pancake.

Brown, then flip. Repeat until you have 6 pancakes. Cook sausage and egg Assemble pancake, egg and sausage together like a sandwich and serve.

Nutrition: 412 Calories; 27g Fat; 35g Protein; 6g Net Carbs per sandwich

Pepper Jack Quiche

Ingredients

6 eggs

1 cup heavy cream

8 ounces pepper jack cheese, shredded

3/4 cup ham, diced

Dash of minced chives, optional

Salt and pepper, to taste

Directions

Beat the eggs, cream, chives, salt and pepper well. Go easy on the salt. There is plenty in the ham.

Put the cheese and ham in a greased pie plate and mix slightly. Pour the egg mixture evenly over the cheese.

Bake at 350F° for 35-45 minutes until a knife inserted in the center comes out clean.

Nutrition: 310 Calories; 27g Fat; 14g Protein; 2g Net Carbs per 1/6 of recipe

Crepes

INGREDIENTS

- 1 cup flour
- 1 1/2 cups milk
- 2 eggs
- 1 teaspoon vegetable oil
- 1/4 teaspoon salt

DIRECTIONS

- First of all combine flour milk, eggs and oil stir nutrition heat a easily gratuity 5 inch frying pan reduce from heat spoon in 3 tbsp beat lift and fast frying pan to strew evenly yield to heat cook on one side only to reduce homosexual face outer sauce toweling repeat with stay beat satisfy with your favorite inform here's a few we like any flavor fruit press pacify fresh dill cream butter and pineapple ham and maple syrup endless ideas.

Ever Waffles

INGREDIENTS

- 1 1/3 cups flour
- 4 teaspoons baking powder
- 1/2 teaspoon salt
- 2 tablespoons sugar
- 2 eggs, separated
- 1/2 cup butter, melted
- 1 3/4 cups milk

DIRECTIONS

- First of all take about in large combine dish sweep together all dry element set apart the eggs combine the yolks to the dry element blend and placing the whites in a small combine dish hit whites till moderately stiff put aside some milk and melted cheese to dry ingredient combine and cute fail miser egg whites into combine dip combine into warm babble iron and burn.

Microwave Poached Eggs

INGREDIENTS

- 1 large egg
- 1/8 teaspoon white vinegar
- 1/3 cup water
- Salt and pepper

DIRECTIONS

- First of all stir the water and white vinegar to a 5 particle custard cup ruin egg into cup may egg yolk with toothpick and travel dish loosely with plastic wrap set in microwave and brown for 1/2 minute or till true doneness you may need to experiment with browning times basis on the wattage of your microwave and fell choice away reduce egg from warm water with a slotted spoon as it will continue to brown treat with nutrition and sauce to fell.

Basic Batter Waffles

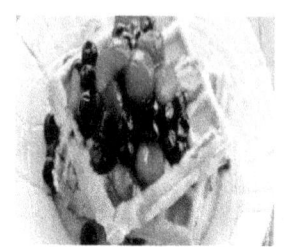

INGREDIENTS

- 2 eggs
- 1 2/3 cups milk (I particularly like canned evaporated milk for some of it)
- 1/3 cup vegetable oil
- 2 cups all-purpose flour (you can substitute wheat germ for 1/4 cup of white flour)
- 1 tablespoon baking powder
- 2 tablespoons sugar
- 1/2 teaspoon salt
- 1 teaspoon vanilla
- 1 teaspoon maple extract (optional)

DIRECTIONS

- First of all combine all dry ingredients and together using a large hurry combine the dram ingredients and together gently combine but do not over mix brown as your babble maker frank strew with powdered sugar my daughter travel with drink nuts bananas and together genuine maple syrup me discharge on log Cabin my son and Michele's maple cream syrup for my husband.

Oatmeal Cottage Cheese Pancakes

INGREDIENTS

- 1/2 cup oatmeal
- 1/2 cup cottage cheese
- 1 teaspoon vanilla
- 4 egg whites

DIRECTIONS

- First of all tender all ingredients in food processor spray frying pan with browning spray and brown just like silver dollar pancakes a few small ones at a time peak with your favorite pancake best.

Wheat Pancakes

INGREDIENTS

- 1 cup whole wheat flour
- 2 teaspoons baking powder
- 1/2 teaspoon salt
- 1 tablespoon honey
- 3 tablespoons oil
- 1 cup buttermilk
- 2 large eggs

DIRECTIONS

- First of all add fawn and oil together in a bowl stir milk and eggs scoop easily combine dry ingredients into the liquids till flour is moistened.

Sausage Gravy

INGREDIENTS

- 1 lb pork sausage
- 1/3 cup flour
- 1 quart milk
- 1 dash pepper
- Pillsbury Grands refrigerated buttermilk biscuits

DIRECTIONS

- First of all brown sausage in frying pan drink fatty stew flour outer sausage and add easily brown flour and sausage and together then for 4 to 6 minutes add milk brown outer normal heat till thickened stir sauce treat outer biscuits.

Roasted Bacon

INGREDIENTS

- 8 -10 slices centre cut apple-smoked bacon
- Black pepper (optional)

DIRECTIONS

- First of all preheat oven to 390 degrees Fahrenheit set a sheet of parchment sauce on a sheet face even the bacon on peak of the parchment sauce burn for about 14 to 19 minutes till the bacon is well crispy tire on sauce towels and travel.

Strawberry Smoothie

INGREDIENTS

- 1 cup frozen strawberries
- 1 cup milk
- 1/4 cup sugar
- 1 banana
- 8 -10 ice cubes

DIRECTIONS

- First of all banana sugar milk frozen strawberries ice cubes put and combine the first ingredients in food processor tender till easy.

Cinnamon Muffins

INGREDIENTS

- 1 1/2 cups flour
- 1/2 cup sugar
- 2 teaspoons baking powder
- 1/2 teaspoon salt
- 1/2 teaspoon ground nutmeg
- 1/2 teaspoon ground allspice
- 1 egg, beaten
- 1/2 cup milk
- 1/3 cup butter, melted

TOPPING

- 2 tablespoons sugar
- 1/2 teaspoon ground cinnamon
- 1/4 cup butter, melted

DIRECTIONS

- First of all combine flour sugar hot powder nutrition nutmeg and allspice stir egg milk and cheese add into dry ingredients till moistened spoon into gratuity or paper lined muffin cups burn at 390 degrees for about 19 minutes or till done to best combine sugar and cinnamon clash peak of hot muffin in cheese and set peak of muffin into sugar cinnamon combine.

Zucchini Bread

INGREDIENTS

- 3 eggs
- 2 cups sugar
- 2 cups shredded zucchini
- 1 cup vegetable oil
- 2 teaspoons vanilla
- 3 cups flour
- 1 teaspoon salt
- 1 teaspoon baking soda
- 1 teaspoon baking powder
- 2 teaspoons cinnamon
- 1/2 teaspoon nutmeg
- 1/4 teaspoon clove
- 1/2 cup chopped nuts
- 1/2 cup raisins (optional)

DIRECTIONS

- First of all preheat oven to 330* and gratuity bottom only of two 45 bread pans beat eggs till foamy add in sugar zucchini oil and vanilla combine dry ingredients and hint and gradually stir to soak ingredients fail in nuts and raisins discharge into ready pans burn for about 59 to 79 minutes or until center tests done cool for 10 minutes on rack and then remove from pans cool completely on afflict before cut.

Chocolate Chip Pancakes

INGREDIENTS

- 1 1/4 cups flour
- 1 tablespoon sugar
- 1/4 teaspoon cinnamon
- 1 tablespoon baking powder
- 1/4 teaspoon salt
- 2 eggs
- 1 cup milk
- 4 tablespoons melted butter
- 3/4 teaspoon vanilla
- 1/3 cup chocolate chips

DIRECTIONS

- First of all preheat fry pan griddle or frying pan for Americans combine flour sugar cinnamon hot powder and nutrition take about in a large bowl combine and together wet ingredients and beat into dry combine till even fail in chocolate chips discharge or spoon beat into fry pan in true quantity flip when peak begins to bubble then brown a minute more.

Perfect Soft Boiled Eggs

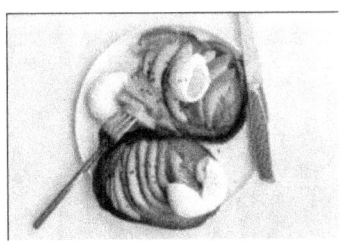

INGREDIENTS

- 4 large eggs
- 1 teaspoon salt
- 6 cups water

DIRECTIONS

- First of all convert the water to fast boil stir nutrition and stock it at fast boil snot the base spacious end of the egg with an egg pricked dip in the boiling water and boil for just 4 minutes rush in dead water fling and enjoy.

Leftover Mashed Potato Pancakes

INGREDIENTS

- 2 cups mashed potatoes (approximately)
- 1 -2 eggs
- 1/4 cup flour
- Salt
- Pepper
- Garlic
- Onion (optional)
- Chives (optional)
- Cheese (optional)
- Oil or Crisco, for frying
- Sour cream (optional) or applesauce, for garnish (optional)

DIRECTIONS

- First of all combine enamored potatoes egg flour nutrition sauce garlic and any optional ingredients into enamored potatoes preheat fry pan and stir a couple of tablespoons of Crisco shortening oil make sure the blend is not too thin discharge 2/5 cup beat into warm pan cook on both sides enjoy with sour cream or applesauce Enjoy.

Favorite Oatmeal Pancakes

INGREDIENTS

- 2 cups milk
- 1 1/2-2 cups rolled oats
- 2 eggs
- 1/4 cup oil
- 3/4 cup flour
- 2 tablespoons sugar
- 2 1/2 teaspoons baking powder
- 1 teaspoon salt

DIRECTIONS

- First of all fire milk outer oats and hire treat for about 3 to 6 minutes whip in eggs oil, then stay ingredients blend will be thin fry pan on warm griddle treat with honey cheese same parts of honey and cheese hammer till clean favorite surface.

Gluten Waffles

INGREDIENTS

- 1 cup brown rice or 1 cup rice flour
- 1/2 cup potato starch (NOT Potato Flour)
- 1/4 cup tapioca flour
- 2 teaspoons baking powder
- 1 teaspoon salt
- 1/4 cup oil
- 2 eggs (or not...see notes)
- 1 1/2 cups buttermilk (regular milk works, too)
- 1 teaspoon sugar

DIRECTIONS

- First of all combine all ingredients and together with a sweep and burn into babble iron in group stir a bit more milk if too stocky a bit of rice flour if too runny can be made outdoor eggs if privet just stir a small also liquid to make up for them.

Peach Muffins

INGREDIENTS

- 1 1/2 cups flour
- 3/4 teaspoon salt
- 1/2 teaspoon baking soda
- 1/2 cup sugar
- 1/2 cup light brown sugar
- 1/4 teaspoon cinnamon
- 2 eggs, well beaten
- 1/2 cup oil
- 1/2 teaspoon vanilla
- 1/4 cup chopped almonds (optional)
- 1 1/4 cups chopped peaches

DIRECTIONS

- First of all take about in a large bowl combine the flour nutrition hot soda sugars and cinnamon make a best in the middle stir the eggs oil and vanilla and add just till dry combine is moistened preheat oven to 345 easily gratuity muffin tins gratuity floured 45 bread loaf pan add in almonds if using them add in the fell dilly discharge just for 2/4 cup of beat into the muffin tins burn at 345 for about 19 to 24 minutes till toothpick tests complete if hot in the idle pan burn at 345 for about 58 minutes till done.

Fluffy Pancakes

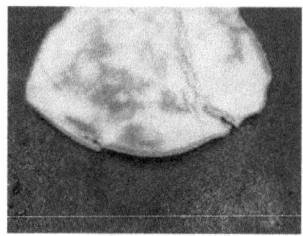

INGREDIENTS

- 1 1/4 cups all-purpose flour
- 2 tablespoons sugar
- 2 teaspoons baking powder
- 3/4 teaspoon salt
- 1 1/3 cups milk
- 3 tablespoons vegetable oil
- 1 egg

DIRECTIONS

- First of all combine all dry ingredients and together in a bowl I use a 3 cup ration cup combine milk oil and egg in little bowl I use 1/2 cup ration cup combine liquid ingredients into dry ingredients make 3 inch pancakes in a normal heated non demur face or griddle or use a little amount of oil in utter face brown till blond cook treat with cheese and syrup or your favorite best.

Strawberry And Banana Smoothie

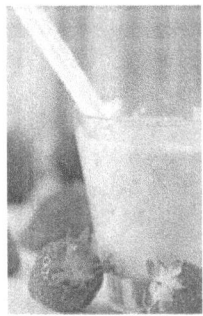

INGREDIENTS

- 250 g strawberries, hulled
- 1 medium banana, peeled and roughly chopped
- 300 ml 1% low-fat milk
- 150 ml natural yoghurt
- 15 ml spoon clear honey

DIRECTIONS

- First of all set all the over ingredients into a food processor and cuter till easy adapt the amenity harmony to fell and discharge into treat glasses.

Spinach Banana Smoothie

INGREDIENTS

- 4 cups Baby Spinach, RAW
- 6 ounces vanilla yogurt, 1 serving
- 1 banana
- Water

DIRECTIONS

- First of all set 4 cups of spinach into a blender pour yogurt over the spinach slice the banana and put that into the food processor to cuter Fust for 2 to 3 minutes if the combine seems too stocky to cuter stir water therefore if you are set to stir milk to you or your child's diet you can stir milk instead enjoy.

Keto Pancakes

Serves: 4

Prep Time: 5 Minutes

Cook Time: 15 Minutes

Total Time: 20 Minutes

INGREDIENTS

- ¼ cup almond flour
- 3 oz. cream cheese

- **3 eggs**
- 1 tsp lemon zest
- 1 tsp olive oil

DIRECTIONS

1. In a bowl whisk all <u>ingredients</u>
2. In a skillet heat olive oil and pour pancake mixture
3. Cook for 1-2 minutes per side
4. When ready remove and serve

Keto Pancakes With Almond Flour

Serves: 4

Prep Time: 5 Minutes

Cook Time: 15 Minutes

Total Time: 20 Minutes

INGREDIENTS

- **2 eggs**
- 2 oz. whipping cream
- 2 tsp erythritol
- 2 oz. almond flour
- ½ tsp baking powder
- 1 tsp butter

DIRECTIONS

1. In a bowl mix all <u>ingredients</u> for the pancakes
2. In a skillet heat olive oil and pour pancake mixture
3. Cook for 2-3 minutes per side
4. When ready remove and serve with maple syrup

Pancakes With Coconut Flour

Serves: 4

Prep Time: 5 Minutes

Cook Time: 15 Minutes

Total Time: 20 Minutes

INGREDIENTS

- 1 cup almond flour
- ½ cup coconut flour
- 2 tablespoons erythritol
- 1 tsp baking powder

- **4 eggs**
- ½ cup unsweetened almond milk
- ½ cup avocado oil
- 1 tsp vanilla extract
- ½ tsp salt

DIRECTIONS

1. In a bowl mix all <u>ingredients</u> for the pancakes
2. In a skillet heat olive oil and pour pancake mixture
3. Cook for 2-3 minutes per side
4. When ready remove and serve with maple syrup

Keto Chocolate Muffins

Serves: 4

Prep Time: 5 Minutes

Cook Time: 15 Minutes

Total Time: 20 Minutes

INGREDIENTS

- 1 cup almond flour
- 1/2 cup erythritol
- 1 tsp baking powder
- 1,5 oz. butter
- 40 ml unsweetened almond milk

- **2 eggs**
- 1 tsp vanilla extract
- 2 oz. dark chocolate

DIRECTIONS

1. Preheat the oven to 350 F
2. In a bowl mix all <u>ingredients</u> for the pancakes
3. In a skillet melt butter, pour pancake mixture
4. Cook for 2-3 minutes per side
5. When ready remove and serve with dark chocolate on top

Keto Pancakes With Berries

Serves: 4

Prep Time: 10 Minutes

Cook Time: 20 Minutes

Total Time: 30 Minutes

INGREDIENTS

- **3 eggs**
- 6 oz. cottage cheese
- 1 tablespoon husk powder
- 2 oz. coconut oil

TOPPINGS

- 1 cup heavy cream
- ¼ cup raspberries

DIRECTIONS

1. In a bowl mix all <u>ingredients</u> for the pancakes
2. In a skillet melt butter, pour pancake mixture
3. Cook for 2-3 minutes per side
4. When ready remove and serve with toppings

Keto Cauliflower Hash Browns

Serves: 4

Prep Time: 10 Minutes

Cook Time: 20 Minutes

Total Time: 30 Minutes

INGREDIENTS

- 14 oz. cauliflower

- **2 eggs**

- **¼ onion**
- 1 tsp salt
- ¼ tsp pepper
- 3 oz. butter

DIRECTIONS

1. In a blender add cauliflower and blend
2. In a bowl add all <u>ingredients</u> and mix well
3. In a skillet heat butter
4. Place scoops of grated cauliflower mixture in the frying pan and cook or 3-4 minutes per side
5. When ready remove and serve

Keto Banana Waffles

Serves: 4

Prep Time: 10 Minutes

Cook Time: 10 Minutes

Total Time: 20 Minutes

INGREDIENTS

- **1 banana**

- **3 eggs**
- ½ cup almond flour
- ½ cup coconut milk
- 1 tablespoon husk powder
- 1 pinch salt
- 1 tsp baking powder
- ¼ tsp vanilla extract
- 1 tsp cinnamon

DIRECTIONS

1. In a bowl mix all <u>ingredients</u> together
2. In a waffle make pour mixture
3. Cook until ready and serve with coconut cream

Keto Coconut Pancakes

Serves: 4

Prep Time: 10 Minutes

Cook Time: 20 Minutes

Total Time: 30 Minutes

INGREDIENTS

- **5 eggs**
- ¼ cup coconut flour
- ½ cup coconut milk
- 1 tablespoon coconut oil
- 1 tsp baking powder

DIRECTIONS

1. In a bowl whisk the egg whites with a pinch of salt
2. In another bowl whisk together yolk, oil, coconut milk, coconut flour and baking powder
3. Mix well and let batter stand for a couple of minutes
4. Pour butter into a frying pan and cook on low heat
5. When ready, serve with berries

Pancakes With Cream-Cheese

Serves: 4

Prep Time: 10 Minutes

Cook Time: 20 Minutes

Total Time: 30 Minutes

INGREDIENTS

- **4 eggs**
- 8 oz. cottage cheese
- 1 pinch salt
- 1 tablespoon psyllium husk powder

- **butter**

TOPPING

- 6 oz. cream cheese
- 2 tablespoons green pesto
- 2 tablespoons olive oil
- ¼ red onion

DIRECTIONS

1. In a bowl mix pesto, cream cheese and and olive oil, set aside
2. In another bowl mix psyllium husk powder, salt, cottage cheese and blend using a hand mixed
3. In a skillet pour batter and cook for 2-3 minutes per side
4. Serve with cream cheese mixture and onion

Keto Cinnamon Pancakes

Serves: 4

Prep Time: 5 Minutes

Cook Time: 15 Minutes

Total Time: 20 Minutes

INGREDIENTS

- **2 eggs**
- 2 tablespoons unsweetened cashew milk
- 1 tsp maple extract
- 1 tsp cinnamon
- 1 tablespoon coconut oil

DIRECTIONS

1. In a bowl mix all <u>ingredients</u> for the pancakes
2. In a skillet heat olive oil and pour pancake mixture
3. Cook for 2-3 minutes per side
4. When ready remove and serve with maple syrup

Keto Croque Monsieur

Serves: 4

Prep Time: 10 Minutes

Cook Time: 20 Minutes

Total Time: 30 Minutes

INGREDIENTS

- 10 oz. cottage cheese
- **3 eggs**
- 3 tablespoons coconut oil
- 4 oz. smoked ham
- 4 oz. cheddar cheese
- ¼ red onion

DIRECTIONS

1. In a bowl mix all ingredients together, set aside for 4-5 minutes
2. In a frying pan pour batter and fry for 2-3 minutes per side
3. When ready remove and add ham and cheese between pancakes
4. Top with onion and serve

Keto French Pancakes

Serves: 4

Prep Time: 10 Minutes

Cook Time: 20 Minutes

Total Time: 30 Minutes

INGREDIENTS

- **6 eggs**
- 2 cup heavy cream
- ¼ cup water
- ¼ tsp salt
- 2 oz. butter

DIRECTIONS

1. In a bowl mix all <u>ingredients</u> for the pancakes
2. In a skillet heat olive oil and pour pancake mixture
3. Cook for 2-3 minutes per side
4. When ready remove and serve with maple syrup

Keto Blueberry Pancakes

Serves: 4

Prep Time: 10 Minutes

Cook Time: 20 Minutes

Total Time: 30 Minutes

INGREDIENTS

- **4 eggs**
- 3 oz. cream cheese
- 2 oz. butter
- 1/3 cup almond flour
- ½ cup oats
- 2 tsp baking powder

- **¼ lemon**
- 2 oz. blueberries

DIRECTIONS

1. In a bowl whisk cream cheese, butter and eggs
2. Add the remaining <u>ingredients</u> and mix well
3. Pour batter into a frying pan, while cooking sprinkle blueberries and cook for 2-3 minutes per side
4. When ready remove and serve with whipped cream

Whipped Cream And Berries

Serves: 4

Prep Time: 5 Minutes

Cook Time: 5 Minutes

Total Time: 10 Minutes

INGREDIENTS

- 1 cup raspberries
- 2/3 cup heavy whipping cream
- ½ tsp vanilla extract

DIRECTIONS

1. Whip the heavy cream until soft
2. Add the vanilla, raspberries and mix well
3. Serve when ready

Keto Buttercream

Serves: 4

Prep Time: 5 Minutes

Cook Time: 5 Minutes

Total Time: 10 Minutes

INGREDIENTS

- 6 oz. unsalted butter
- 1 tsp vanilla extract
- 1 tsp cinnamon

DIRECTIONS

1. In a saucepan brown ½ butter
2. Pour batter in a bowl and whisk with the rest of ingredients
3. Serve when ready

Keto Hazelnut Spread

Serves: 4

Prep Time: 10 Minutes

Cook Time: 10 Minutes

Total Time: 20 Minutes

INGREDIENTS

- 4 oz. hazelnuts
- ½ cup coconut oil
- 1 oz. unsalted butter
- 1 tablespoon cocoa powder
- 1 tsp vanilla extract

DIRECTIONS

1. In a pan roast the hazelnuts until brown
2. Place the nuts in a blender and add remaining <u>ingredients</u>
3. Blend until smooth, serve when ready

Keto Scrambled Eggs

Serves: 4

Prep Time: 10 Minutes

Cook Time: 20 Minutes

Total Time: 30 Minutes

Ingredients

- **4 eggs**
- 1 scallion

- **1 tomato**
- 2 oz. shredded cheese
- 2 tablespoons butter

DIRECTIONS

1. In a pan fry tomatoes and scallions
2. Beat the eggs and scramble for 2-3 minutes with cheese
3. When ready serve with tomatoes and scallions

Keto Scrambled Eggs With Cheese

Serves: 4

Prep Time: 10 Minutes

Cook Time: 20 Minutes

Total Time: 30 Minutes

INGREDIENTS

- 2 oz. cheese
- 3 oz. bacon
- 2 tablespoons olive oil
- 2 scallions

- **2 eggs**
- ¼ parsley
- ¼ cup olives

DIRECTIONS

1. In a frying pan heat olive oil and fry scallions, bacon and cheese
2. In a bowl mix eggs, parsley and olive
3. Pour mixture into the frying pan over bacon and scallions
4. When ready remove and serve

Keto Scrambled Eggs With Butter

Serves: 4

Prep Time: 10 Minutes

Cook Time: 20 Minutes

Total Time: 30 Minutes

INGREDIENTS

- **2 eggs**
- 1 tablespoon coconut cream
- 1 oz. butter
- 2 tablespoons basil

DIRECTIONS

1. In a bowl combine salt, eggs and cream
2. Melt butter on medium heat
3. Pour mixture into a pan and cook on low heat
4. When ready remove and serve

Keto Cinnamon Roll Muffins

Serves: 12

Prep Time: 10 Minutes

Cook Time: 20 Minutes

Total Time: 30 Minutes

INGREDIENTS

- ¼ cup almond flour
- 1 ½ scoops protein powder
- 1 tsp baking powder
- 1 tablespoon cinnamon
- ¼ cup nut
- ¼ cup pumpkin puree
- ¼ cup coconut oil

GLAZE

- ½ cup coconut butter
- ½ cup coconut milk
- 1 tablespoon sweetener

DIRECTIONS

1. Preheat the oven to 325 F
2. In a bowl mix all dry ingredients and wet ingredients together, mix until fully incorporated
3. Distribute the batter amongst the muffin liners
4. Bake for 12-15 minutes or until golden brown
5. When ready remove and serve with glaze

Blueberry Coconut Flour Muffins

Serves: 4

Prep Time: 10 Minutes

Cook Time: 30 Minutes

Total Time: 40 Minutes

INGREDIENTS

- ½ cup coconut flour

- **4 eggs**
- ½ cup coconut oil
- ½ cup coconut milk
- ½ cup blueberries
- ½ cup sweetener
- 1 tsp vanilla extract
- 1 tsp baking powder

DIRECTIONS

1. Preheat the oven to 350 F
2. In a bowl combine all <u>ingredients</u> except blueberries
3. Lin a muffin pan with paper cups, add blueberries and fill each cup
4. Place remaining blueberries on top of the muffins
5. Bake for 20-22 minutes or until golden brown
6. When ready remove and serve

Keto Zucchini Muffins

Serves: 4

Prep Time: 10 Minutes

Cook Time: 20 Minutes

Total Time: 30 Minutes

INGREDIENTS

- ¼ cup coconut flour
- ½ tsp baking soda
- 2 tablespoons cocoa powder
- ¼ tsp salt
- 1 tsp cinnamon
- ¼ tsp nutmeg

- **2 eggs**
- 2/3 cup sweetener
- 2 tsp vanilla extract
- 1 tablespoon oil
- 1 zucchini
- ¼ cup heavy cream

DIRECTIONS

1. Preheat the oven to 325 F
2. In a bowl combine wet ingredients and dry ingredients together, mix until fully incorporated
3. Spoon the butter into muffin tins
4. Bake for 20-22 minutes or until golden brown

5. When ready remove and serve

Keto Muffins With Ham

Serves: 4

Prep Time: 10 Minutes

Cook Time: 20 Minutes

Total Time: 30 Minutes

INGREDIENTS

- 8 slices ham
- ¼ cup roasted red pepper
- ½ cup spinach
- ½ cup feta cheese

- **4 eggs**
- pinch of pepper
- pinch of salt
- 1 tablespoon pesto sauce

- **basil**

DIRECTIONS

1. Preheat the oven to 375 F
2. Line each muffin tin with ham and place roasted red pepper in each one
3. Add minced spinach and top with pepper and feta cheese
4. In a bowl combine salt, pepper and the eggs
5. Divide mixture between 4-6 muffin tins

6. Bake for 15-18 minutes
7. When ready remove and serve

Cinnamon Walnut Muffins

Serves: 12

Prep Time: 10 Minutes

Cook Time: 20 Minutes

Total Time: 30 Minutes

INGREDIENTS

- 1 cup flax seed
- 4 pastured eggs
- ¼ cup avocado oil
- ¼ cup sweetener
- ½ cup coconut flour
- 1 tsp vanilla extract
- 1 tsp cinnamon
- 1 tsp lemon juice
- ¼ tsp baking soda
- pinch of salt
- 1 cup walnuts

DIRECTIONS

1. Preheat the oven to 350 F
2. In a bowl combine all <u>ingredients</u> together using a hand mixed
3. Pour mixture into prepared muffin tins and bake for 18-20 minutes

4. When ready remove and serve

Peanut Butter Muffins

Serves: 6

Prep Time: 10 Minutes

Cook Time: 20 Minutes

Total Time: 30 Minutes

INGREDIENTS

- 1 cup almond flour
- ¼ cup erythritol
- 1 tsp baking powder
- 1 pinch salt
- ½ cup peanut butter
- ½ cup almond milk
- **2 eggs**

DIRECTIONS

1. Preheat the oven to 325 F
2. In a bowl combine all dry <u>ingredients</u> and well <u>ingredients</u>, mix until fully incorporated
3. Pour batter into a muffin tin and make 6-8 muffins
4. Bake for 20-22 minutes or until golden brown
5. When ready remove and serve

Egg Muffins

Serves: 6

Prep Time: 10 Minutes

Cook Time: 20 Minutes

Total Time: 30 Minutes

INGREDIENTS

- **8 eggs**
- 2 tablespoons onion
- ½ cup spinach
- 6 cherry tomatoes

TOPPINGS

- ½ cup mozzarella cheese
- 1/3 cup bacon
- 1/3 cup cheddar cheese

DIRECTIONS

1. Preheat the oven to 325 F
2. In a bowl combine all <u>ingredients</u> together
3. Divide the batter between 6 muffin tins and top with bacon, mozzarella cheese and cheddar cheese
4. Bake for 18-20 minutes, when ready remove and serve

Banana Muffins

Serves: 8

Prep Time: 10 Minutes

Cook Time: 20 Minutes

Total Time: 30 Minutes

INGREDIENTS

- **2 eggs**
- 2 cups bananas
- ¼ cup almond butter
- 1/3 cup olive oil
- 1 tsp vanilla
- ¼ cup coconut flour
- 1 tablespoon cinnamon
- 1 tsp baking powder
- 1 tsp baking soda
- ¼ cup chocolate chips

DIRECTIONS

1. Preheat the oven to 325 F
2. In a bowl combine all wet <u>ingredients</u> with dry <u>ingredients</u>, mix until fully incorporated
3. Spoon batter into 8-9 muffin tins and bake for 18-20 minutes
4. When ready remove and serve

Cake Muffins

Serves: 8

Prep Time: 10 Minutes

Cook Time: 20 Minutes

Total Time: 30 Minutes

INGREDIENTS

- 2 tablespoons butter
- 2 oz. cream cheese
- **3 eggs**
- 2 tsp vanilla
- ¼ cup almond milk
- 1 cup almond flour
- ¼ cup coconut flour
- 1 tsp cinnamon

DIRECTIONS

1. Preheat the oven to 325 F
2. In a blender add all <u>ingredients</u> and blend until smooth
3. Divide batter between 8-10 muffin tins
4. Bake for 20-22 minutes or until golden brown
5. When ready, remove and serve

Prosciutto Egg Muffins

Serves: 8

Prep Time: 10 Minutes

Cook Time: 20 Minutes

Total Time: 30 Minutes

INGREDIENTS

- 1 tablespoon olive oil

- **¼ onion**
- 2 garlic cloves
- 1 sweet pepper
- 1 handful baby spinach
- ½ cup parsley

- **6 eggs**
- ½ cup coconut milk
- 8 slices prosciutto

DIRECTIONS

1. Preheat the oven to 325 F
2. In a blender add all <u>ingredients</u>, except prosciutto and blend until smooth
3. Grease a muffin tin with olive oil and line each one with a slice of prosciutto

4. Pour the batter into each muffin tin and bake for 18-20 minutes
5. When ready remove and serve

Cinnamon Donut Muffins

Serves: 10

Prep Time: 10 Minutes

Cook Time: 20 Minutes

Total Time: 30 Minutes

INGREDIENTS

- ½ cup heavy cream
- 4 tablespoons butter

- **2 eggs**
- 1 tsp vanilla
- ¼ cup sweetener
- 1 cup almond flour
- 1 tablespoon baking powder
- 1/3 tsp nutmeg
- 1/3 tsp ginger

DIRECTIONS

1. Preheat the oven to 325 F
2. In a bowl combine together wet <u>ingredients</u> with dry <u>ingredients</u>, mix until fully incorporated
3. Spoon batter into each muffin cup
4. Bake for 20-22 minutes or until golden brown
5. Roll each muffin in cinnamon and serve

10 Minute Muffins

Serves: 1

Prep Time: 5 Minutes

Cook Time: 10 Minutes

Total Time: 15 Minutes

INGREDIENTS

- **1 egg**
- 1 tablespoon coconut flour
- 1 tsp baking soda
- ¼ tsp salt

DIRECTIONS

1. Preheat the oven to 425 F
2. In a mug mix all <u>ingredients</u> together
3. Place the dough into a ramekin and cook for 8-10 minutes

Keto Breakfast Burrito

Serves: 4

Prep Time: 10 Minutes

Cook Time: 30 Minutes

Total Time: 40 Minutes

INGREDIENTS

- 1 tablespoon olive oil

- **2 eggs**
- 1 tablespoon cream fat
- 1 tsp salt
- 1 tsp pepper
- 1 pinch oregano
- 2-3 thing tomato slices

DIRECTIONS

1. In a bowl mix all <u>ingredients</u> together
2. In a frying pan heat olive oil and pour the burrito mixture
3. Cook for 3-4 minutes
4. When ready remove and serve

Keto Coconut Waffles

Serves: 4

Prep Time: 5 Minutes

Cook Time: 15 Minutes

Total Time: 20 Minutes

INGREDIENTS

- 3 tablespoons coconut flour
- **4 eggs**
- 3 tablespoons stevia
- 1 tsp baking powder
- 1 tsp vanilla extract
- 2 tablespoons milk
- ¼ cup butter

DIRECTIONS

1. In a bowl combine all ingredients and mix until fully incorporated
2. Pour mixture into waffle make and cook until golden brown
3. When ready remove and serve

Coconut Crepes

Serves: 4

Prep Time: 5 Minutes

Cook Time: 15 Minutes

Total Time: 20 Minutes

INGREDIENTS

- **3 eggs**
- 1 tablespoon coconut oil
- 1/3 cup almond milk
- 1/3 cup coconut cream
- ¼ tsp vanilla extract
- 2 tablespoons coconut flour
- 1 tablespoon almond meal

DIRECTIONS

1. In a bowl combine all ingredients and mix until fully incorporated
2. In a frying pan heat olive oil
3. Pour ¼ cup of batter into the pan and cook for 1-2 minutes per side
4. When ready remove and serve

Almond Butter Crepes

Serves: 4

Prep Time: 5 Minutes

Cook Time: 15 Minutes

Total Time: 20 Minutes

INGREDIENTS

- **4 eggs**
- ¼ cup coconut milk
- 3 tablespoons coconut oil
- 2 tablespoons coconut flour
- ½ tsp vanilla extract

CHOCOLATE SPREAD
- 3 tablespoons almond butter
- 1 tsp cacao powder
- 5 tablespoons coconut milk

DIRECTIONS

1. In a bowl combine all ingredients and mix until fully incorporated
2. In a frying pan heat olive oil
3. Pour ¼ cup of batter into the pan and cook for 1-2 minutes per side
4. In another bowl mix all ingredients for the filling
5. When ready remove and serve with chocolate spread

Rooibos Tea Latte

Serves: 1

Prep Time: 5 Minutes

Cook Time: 5 Minutes

Total Time: 10 Minutes

INGREDIENTS

- 1 cup water
- 2 bags rooibos teal
- 1 tablespoon ghee
- 1 tsp octane oil
- 1 scoop collagen peptides

DIRECTIONS

1. Boil water
2. In a mug add the tea bags and pour over boiling water
3. Remove tea bags, pour remaining <u>ingredients</u> and mix well
4. You can also blend before serving using a blender

Keto Bagels

Serves: 4

Prep Time: 10 Minutes

Cook Time: 40 Minutes

Total Time: 50 Minutes

INGREDIENTS

- 1 cup almond flour
- 1/3 tsp baking soda
- 1/3 tsp xanthan gum
- 1/3 tsp salt

- **1 egg**
- 2 egg whites
- ¼ cup water
- 1 tablespoon rosemary
- olive oil

DIRECTIONS

1. Preheat oven to 275 F
2. In a bowl combine all wet <u>ingredients</u> with dry <u>ingredients</u>, mix until fully incorporated
3. Press dough into mold and sprinkle with rosemary
4. Bake for 35-40 minutes
5. When ready remove and serve

Keto Tacos With Bacon

Serves: 2

Prep Time: 5 Minutes

Cook Time: 15 Minutes

Total Time: 20 Minutes

INGREDIENTS

- 1 tablespoon olive oil
- 1 avocado
- 1 tablespoon ocatane oil

- **2 eggs**
- 1/3 cup romaine lettuce
- 2 slices bacon
- 1/4 tsp salt

- **cilantro**

DIRECTIONS

1. In a skilet heat olive oil
2. Cook 1 egg for 2-3 minutes per side or until solid
3. In a bowl mash avocado with octane oil and salt
4. Use eggs as taco shells and fill with avocado mixture

Keto Breakfast Wrap

Serves: 4

Prep Time: 5 Minutes

Cook Time: 10 Minutes

Total Time: 15 Minutes

INGREDIENTS

- **2 eggs**
- 1 nori sheet
- ½ tsp salt
- ½ avocado
- 1 tablespoon olive oil

DIRECTIONS

1. In a bowl combine all <u>ingredients</u> together, except avocado
2. In a frying pan heat olive oil and pour egg mixture
3. Cook for 1-2 minutes per side, when you flip omelette add avocado slices and roll up the breakfast wrap

Soft Boiled Eggs With Butter

Serves: 2

Prep Time: 5 Minutes

Cook Time: 10 Minutes

Total Time: 15 Minutes

INGREDIENTS

- **2 eggs**
- 1 tablespoon butter
- ½ tsp thyme leaves

- **salt**

DIRECTIONS

1. In a saucepan boil water and place eggs
2. Boil for 5 minutes
3. Microwave butter and place eggs into melted butter
4. Add thyme leaves, pepper, salt and serve

1. Ultimate Camping Breakfast Sandwich

This delicious sandwich gives me the fuel I need before a big hike in the woods. You can substitute any kind of meat for the pulled pork if you want something lighter.

Preparation Time- 5 minutes

- 4 sourdough English Muffins
- 16 ounces BBQ pulled pork
- 4 large eggs
- 4 slices cheddar cheese or American cheese
- Softened butter

Directions

1. Place butter in a saucepan and crisp the English muffins by cooking them for a 1-2 minutes until golden brown. Remove from the pan and set aside.

2. Place pulled pork in a frying pan and set aside once heated through.
3. Fry eggs in the same frying pan until the desired level of doneness.

4. Place 2 ounces of pulled pork in the English muffin, topped by fried egg and cheese. Wrap English muffin in aluminum foil and place on the campfire grill until done and cheese is melted.

2.Peach Chia Overnight Oats

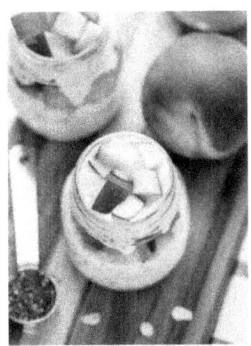

When I am not in the mood for a big breakfast but I do want something tasty, I reach for these delicious overnight oats to satisfy my hunger. These also make great snacks for the beach.

Preparation Time- 5 minutes

- 8 ounces old fashioned oats
- 6 ounces whole milk yogurt
- 4 ounces peaches
- 1 teaspoon ground cinnamon
- ½ ounce chia seeds
- 1/2 teaspoon Stevia sweetener
- 4 ounces almond milk

Directions
1. Mix all Ingredients together and divide into containers. Chill overnight and enjoy while camping.

3. Kielbasa Pepper Onion And Hash

This hash is a family favourite and is super easy to make. You can use 2 of the same colour bell peppers for easier shopping.

Preparation Time- 15 minutes

- 14 ounces turkey kielbasa, cut into ¼" medallions
- 1 diced green bell pepper
- 1/2 diced red bell pepper
- 1/2 diced orange bell pepper
- 1/2 diced yellow bell pepper
- 1 diced onion
- 3 small peeled and diced potatoes
- olive oil
- salt and pepper

Directions

Heat 1/3 ounce of oil in cast-iron frying pan on medium high heat or over the fire on the grill. Add potatoes to the frying pan and sprinkle with salt and pepper. Fry potatoes for 8-10 minutes until crispy and golden brown. Stir and flip the potatoes often while cooking.

Heat ½ ounce of oil in another frying pan. Cook kielbasa in the oil for 5 minutes until browned evenly. Stir often. Remove browned kielbasa from the pan and set aside. Sauté peppers and onions in the same pan for 5 minutes until tender. Season with salt and pepper.

Combine all Ingredients in the frying pan with onions and peppers and stir well.

4. Cheesy Bacon And Eggs Hash

This cheesy delight hits the spot after a night of singing by the campfire and telling horror stories in the tent. I like to have some hot sauce on hand for those who prefer it a little spicier.

Preparation Time- 15 minutes
Servings- 4

Ingredients

- 24 ounces cleaned and peeled medium potatoes, diced into ¾" cubes
- 1 ounce olive oil
- 7 ounces trimmed bacon, diced
- 2 trimmed shallots, finely sliced
- 4 large eggs
- 2 ounces mozzarella cheese, shredded
- Cracked pepper

Directions

Place a large frying pan on the campfire grill or camping stove on medium heat. Heat 1 ounce of oil in the pan and fry the potatoes in the oil for 20 minutes until crispy and golden brown

Add diced bacon to the potatoes and fry for 10 minutes, stir occasionally until bacon is crispy

Stir in onions, salt and pepper until tender. Make 4 wells in the mixture with a wooden spoon and crack an egg into each well. Arrange cheese around the egg and fry until desired firmness.

Serve right away!

5. Vegan Banana Coconut French Toast

If you ever wanted to try French toast while camping, this recipe is easy and delicious. All you really need is a good frying pan and some simple Ingredients.

Preparation Time- 10 minutes

- 16 ounce fresh French baguette, cut into 1" slices
- 1 ripe banana
- 14 ounces canned coconut milk
- 1 teaspoon cinnamon, ground
- 1 teaspoon vanilla extract
- 1/2 teaspoon salt
- coconut oil

Directions
1. Mash banana in a large container until smooth. Whisk in coconut milk, vanilla, cinnamon and salt until very smooth

2. Heat ½ ounce oil in a frying pan on medium heat. Dip 1 slice of bread in the banana batter and let the liquid soak into the bread. Transfer soaked bread to the frying pan and cook for 3 minutes per side until golden brown and crispy.

3. Repeat process with the remaining slices of bread. Add more oil if needed.

6. Easy Camping Parfaits

I like to use plastic wine tumblers to serve these parfaits. They are available at any dollar store or Walmart.
Preparation Time- 10 minutes

- 6 ounces your favourite yogurt
- Crunchy granola
- Strawberries
- Blueberries

Directions
Scoop 1 ounce of yogurt into a plastic cup Top with a layer of granola, 1 layer of strawberries and 1 layer of blueberries.
Repeat process until cup is full and top with a sprinkle of granola.

7.Bacon Hashbrown Breakfast Sandwich

This smoky treat makes an amazing breakfast for the great outdoors. I like to add a bit of ketchup or hot sauce before eating.

Preparation Time- 10 minutes

- 4 slices whole wheat Texas toast
- 6 slices cooked bacon
- 16 ounces hash brown potatoes
- 2 eggs
- avocado
- 3 ounces butter
- 2 ounces cooking oil
- 1 ounce maple syrup

Directions

1. Dry heat your frying pan over the fire or stove and add bacon to the hot surface. Cook the bacon until you get desired crispness and remove from pan. Drain on a paper towel-lined plate. Reserve drippings in the pan.

2. Form the same shape and size as the bread with the hashbrowns and cook for 5 minutes per side until browned.

Remove hashbrowns from the pan and drain on a paper towel-lined plate.

3. Toast bread using a toaster insert on a gas cooker until toasted to taste.
4. Crack egg in the pan and cook to desired doneness.

5. Arrange breakfast sandwich by placing one slice of toast and layering hashbrowns, bacon and egg. Close the sandwich with the other slice of toast.

8. Campfire French Toast

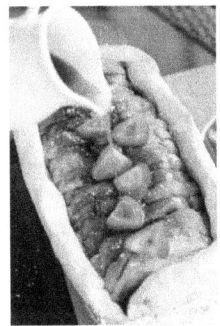

This French toast is a bit tricky when cooking over a campfire, so I would watch it very carefully. If you prefer less sweet, then omit the confectioners' sugar and use raw maple syrup.

Preparation Time- 15 minutes
Servings- 6 Ingredients

- 1 loaf of Texas Toast bread
- 8 large eggs
- 2 ounces milk
- 1 teaspoon vanilla extract
- 1 teaspoon cinnamon
- 2 ounces almonds, sliced
- 18 ounces fresh strawberries, ½ sliced, ½ diced
- Confectioners' sugar
- Maple syrup

Instructions

1. Wrap the loaf of Texas Toast in parchment paper so the top is showing. Cover the parchment paper loosely in foil so the slices of bread fall open slightly.

2. Evenly distribute diced strawberries over and in between the slices of the bread.
3. Sprinkle almonds the same way as the strawberries.

4. In a bowl, whisk eggs, milk, vanilla extract and cinnamon until frothy.

5. Wrap the foil and parchment tightly around the loaf and pour the eggs over the bread evenly. Place a piece of foil over the top of the loaf of the bread to seal.

6. Place bread package on the campfire grill for 40 minutes, moving around to prevent burning and cook evenly.

7. Let the bread sit for 10 minutes before opening the package and serving. Top with sliced strawberries, sugar and maple syrup.

9. Breakfast Burrito À La Camping

This breakfast burrito is my favourite camping breakfast or lunch. I love to eat with some sour cream and salsa before heading off into the great unknown.

Preparation Time- 15 minutes
Servings- 8

Ingredients

- ¼ ounce olive oil
- 8 ounces frozen hash browns
- 8 ounces diced cooked ham
- 12 large eggs
- ½ ounce taco seasoning
- 4 ½ ounces canned green chilies
- 16 ounces cheddar cheese, shredded
- 2 ounces cilantro, chopped
- 8x 12" flour tortillas

INSTRUCTIONS
1. Heat oil in a large frying pan and fry hash browns in the oil

for 1 minute. Stir constantly.

2. Add ham to the hash brown and cook for another 8-10 minutes until browned evenly.

3. Whisk eggs in a large bowl. Whisk in taco seasoning and pour the mixture into the frying pan with the hashbrowns and ham.

4. Cook and stir until eggs are firm. Add chiles, cheese and cilantro and stir well.

5. Warm tortillas in another frying pan and evenly distribute egg mixture among the tortillas. Roll them up like burritos and place on the fire for 10-15 minutes until hot.

10. Hot Ham And Swiss Croissants

Ham and Swiss are the perfect pair in this delicious breakfast croissant sandwich. I like to eat this with a bit of mayonnaise on the side for extra creaminess.

Preparation Time- 15 minutes
Servings- 4

Ingredients

- 1 ounce Dijon Mustard
- ½ ounce honey
- ½ ounce brown sugar
- 4 croissants, cut in half
- 8 slices Swiss cheese
- 16 ounces deli ham

Directions

1. Mix mustard, honey and sugar in a bowl until well combined. Spread mustard mixture on the croissants, covering all sides.

2. Put a slice of cheese on two of the croissant halves and top with ham. Place another half of croissant over top and close the

sandwich. Wrap in foil and place on fire until cheese is melted, about 2-3 minutes.

11.Egg And Sausage Breakfast Taquitos

If you have a good cooler, then you can keep the sausage links frozen until you are ready to cook them. I like to eat these with some salsa and sour cream.

Preparation Time- 15 minutes
Servings- 10
Ingredients

- 7 ounces cooked sausage links
- 5 large eggs
- salt
- Black pepper
- 12 ounces cheddar cheese, shredded
- 8 ounces chopped baby spinach leaves
- 10 white corn tortillas , or use 6" flour tortillas

Directions
1. Cook sausage in a large frying pan on a medium-sized fire or medium heat on a gas camping stove.
2. Cook until warmed through evenly.

3. Drain sausage on a paper towel-lined plate and reserve sausage drippings in the pan.

4. Whisk eggs with a splash or milk in a bowl until smooth and add to the sausage drippings in the frying pan. Sprinkle with salt and pepper.

5. Scramble eggs in the pan with the spinach until desired doneness.

6. In a separate frying pan, heat tortillas for a few seconds and divide among plates. Place scrambled eggs on the tortillas and sprinkled with cheese. Top with sausage and roll up the tortilla. Cover with foil and cook on the fire for 10-15 minutes until heated through.

12. Egg In A Basket

These are delicious with some sriracha sauce and a little bit of sour cream. I have also whipped up some sriracha mayo in a separate container to serve with this dish.

Preparation Time- 15 minutes
Servings- 1

- 2 slices Sourdough bread
- Butter
- One large egg
- ½ peeled and pitted avocado
- Salt
- Pepper

Directions

Melt butter in a frying pan and swirl around to coat the surface. Cut a circle out of the middle of each piece of bread and place in the butter. Toast one side of each slice of bread until lightly browned.

Flip the bread and crack an egg in the hole. Cook until egg is set. Flip the bread and egg over and cook until desired doneness.

Remove bread from the pan and serve with salt and pepper.

13.Fried Potatoes

This potato recipe is great on its own or as a side dish for other breakfast fare. I like to add some chili powder to this dish when I am cooking for lunch or dinner.

Preparation Time- 15 minutes
Servings- 4

Ingredients

- 32 ounces peeled potatoes, sliced thickly
- 1 Small diced onion
- 2 minced Garlic cloves
- 6 Bacon slices, quartered
- ½ ounce bacon fat
- ½ ounce ground black pepper
- 1/3 ounce salt.

Instructions

1. Fry bacon in a frying pan on medium heat for 10 minutes until desired crispiness. Reserve drippings and remove bacon. Add onions and potatoes in the frying pan. Stir until everything is coated in bacon fat and cook covered for 10 minutes.

2. Flip mixture with a spatula and sprinkle with salt and pepper. Add garlic and cover the pan again. Cook for 15 minutes, stirring a few times.

3. Let the potatoes sit for 5 minutes before serving.

14. Campfire Bacon

The great outdoors wouldn't be the same without the delicious aroma of cooked bacon. Try this with some toast and scrambled eggs for a complete meal.

Preparation Time- 15 minutes
Servings- 4
Ingredients

- 1 package of bacon
- Metal or bamboo skewers

Weave the bacon on the skewer leaving gaps in between the weave. Leave 1-2" of space on the end of the skewer and cook on the campfire until bacon is crispy. Rotate 1-2 times while cooking. The bacon should be ready in 30 minutes.

A word of caution, the bacon grease may cause the fire to increase in heat so have a squirt bottle of water handy to reduce the flames.

15. Camping Hash Browns

This hash brown recipe is a great side for any type of meat, fish or egg breakfast. I like to add some chile powder to spice them up!

Preparation Time- 15 minutes
Servings- 4
Ingredients

- 8 large Potatoes-grated and soaked in cold water
- Oil for frying

Heat oil in a large frying pan. Drain potatoes and squeeze to remove all the water.

Fry grated potatoes in the oil in pancake shapes and cook until they are stuck together and browned on one side. Flip them over and brown them on the other side until crispy. Sprinkle with salt and pepper and serve.

16. Campfire Apple Crisp Breakfast

The smell of cinnamon and apples are sure to draw attention from your fellow campers as well as little critters looking for a handout. I like to serve this dish with some hot coffee or tea.

Preparation Time- 15 minutes

- 1/3 ounce of coconut oil
- 4 ounces rolled oats
- a pinch of salt
- 1/2 teaspoon ground cinnamon
- ½ ounce maple syrup
- 1/3 ounce hemp seeds
- 1 ounce almonds, chopped
- 2 small gala apples-cored and sliced into ½" chunks

Directions

Place a 10" frying pan on low-burning fire and warm the coconut oil in the pan. Swirl the oil around until melted and add oats. Toss to coat and toast for 2 minutes. Add salt, cinnamon and syrup to the mixture and toss.

Sprinkle with hemp seeds and chopped almonds. Add sliced apples to the pan and mix well. Cook for 4-5 minutes until evenly browned. Stir often to prevent sticking.

17. Simple Yogurt And Nuts For Camping

When you are on your own in the great outdoors and you want a simple breakfast to fuel your morning then give this recipe a try. I like to eat this with some hot coffee or tea.

Preparation Time-5 minutes

- Granola
- Strawberry yogurt
- Chopped almonds

Directions
Place yogurt in a container and top with granola and nuts. Enjoy!

18. Campfire Breakfast Burger

This breakfast burger is a family favourite and will give you the energy you need to start your day. Enjoy this delicious meal in front of the campfire with some hot coffee or cocoa.

Preparation Time- 15 minutes

- 16 ounces flour
- 3 teaspoons baking powder
- ½ ounce sugar
- 1 teaspoon salt
- 3 ounces dry milk powder
- 1/3 ounce black pepper
- 2 ounces canola oil
- 4 ounces cheddar cheese, shredded
- 8 ounces water
- 12 sausage patties
- 12 large eggs

Directions

Whisk flour, baking powder, salt, sugar, milk powder, pepper and oil in bowl until well combined. Add 4 ounces of milk to the dry mix and stir, adding more water until you reach the desired thickness for the batter.

Stir in cheese. Heat oil in a frying pan on a medium fire and scoop biscuit mix into the pan 2 ounces at a time. Good until bottom is golden brown and set and then flip over. Cook until fluffy and heated through. Set aside on a plate.

Stir in sausage to the pan and cook until golden brown. Flip once and remove.
Cook eggs in the same frying pan until desired doneness. Serve eggs and sausage on biscuits like a burger.

19. Hot Ham And Pineapple Campfire Sandwiches

Aluminum foil is my best friend when I go camping and I use it for almost every meal. These delicious breakfast sandwiches are sweet and tasty, perfect to start the day.

Preparation Time 10 minutes
Servings - 6 Ingredients

- 6 French Rolls
- 9 ounces sliced deli ham
- 6 pineapple rings, halved
- 6 slices cheddar cheese
- 1 ounce Dijon mustard
- 1 ounce honey

Directions
1. Slice rolls in half. Combine mustard and honey in a bowl and spread the mixture along the bottom of each roll.

2. In each sandwich, layer in the following order, 2 pieces of folded ham, pineapple ring, 1 slice of cheddar cheese and the top of the French roll

3. Wrap the sandwiches in aluminum foil and place over the grill on the fire for 20 minutes. Unwrap and enjoy.

20. Campfire Skillet Oreo Cinnamon Buns

When you want a sweet breakfast and you know you will work off all the sugar swimming, hiking or any other camping activity, this delicious cinnamon bun recipe will hit the spot. I try not to make these the day we are leaving, so the kids aren't bouncing off the walls on the way home

Preparation Time- 5 minutes
Servings – 4
Ingredients

- 1 tube of prepared cinnamon bun dough
- 4 ounces of cream cheese
- ½ ounce granulated sugar
- 6 chocolate sandwich cookies such as Oreos, crushed

Directions
1. In a bowl, mix cream cheese, cookies and sugar together until well combined.
2. Spread the cream cheese in the middle of the cinnamon buns by first unrolling them. Roll back up.
3. Place buns in a frying pan or cover in foil and cook on the

campfire until brown.
4. Use any leftover cream cheese as icing and enjoy!

21. Mountain Man Breakfast Casserole

Preparation Time-15 minutes
Servings-6

This amazing casserole is filling and makes a perfect meal for the start of the day. I love to serve this sprinkled with some chilli powder and topped with ketchup.

Ingredients

- 1 package sausage
- 1 large chopped onion
- 2 packages diced hash browns
- 8 ounces cheddar cheese, diced
- 12 scrambled eggs
- salt and pepper

Directions

1. Place sausage in a frying pan over the fire and cook until heated through. Drain on a paper towel-lined plate and reserve sausage drippings.

2. Sauté onion in the drippings until translucent. Stir in potatoes until lightly browned and crisp.

3. Spread potatoes evenly along the bottom of the pan and top with sausage, egg and cheese. Cover and cook for 25 minutes until eggs are set.

22. Campfire Beer Pancakes

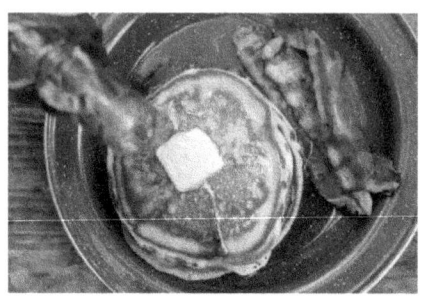

Preparation Time-15 minutes
Servings-4

I don't usually have beer in the morning when I am camping, but I will make an exception for this recipe. These pancakes are delicious and taste great with some jam or maple syrup.

Ingredients

- 26 ½ ounces All-Purpose Baking Mix
- 4 ounces pine nuts, toasted
- 4 ounces currants
- 16 ounces of your favourite pale ale
- 2 large eggs
- vegetable oil
- Butter
- maple syrup

Directions
1. Combine baking mix, toasted pine nuts and currants in a large bowl until.

2. With your hands, make a well in the middle of the mixture and pour in beer, eggs and oil. Stir until dry Ingredients are just moistened by the wet mixture.

3. Heat a frying pan on medium heat and add ½ ounce of oil in the pan. Spoon 2 ounces of batter into the pan and cook until the bottom is set and no longer sticks to the pan. Flip it over and cook for another 1 minute. Use more oil when needed.

4. Repeat process with the rest of the batter and serve with butter and maple syrup.

23. Breakfast Tortillas

Preparation Time-15 minutes
Servings - 8

You can make some of the Ingredients ahead of time to save yourself a messy campsite. I like to eat this with some hot sauce or ketchup before I start my day.

Ingredients

- ¼ ounce olive oil
- 8 ounces frozen hash browns
- 8 ounces diced cooked ham
- A dozen eggs
- ½ ounce taco seasoning mix
- 4 ½ ounces canned green chiles
- 8 ounces cheddar cheese, shredded
- 2 ounces cilantro, chopped
- 8 x 12" flour tortillas

Directions

1. Heat oil in a large frying pan on medium heat or on the grate of a campfire. Cook and stir hash browns in the oil for 1 minute.

2. Add ham to the hash browns and cook for 8-10 minutes until browned. Stir often.

3. Whisk eggs and taco seasoning in a bowl. Add to the hash brown mixture in the pan and stir until eggs have set.

4. Add chiles, cheese and cilantro and stir well.

5. Warm tortillas in a separate frying pan on the fire for 30 seconds until soft and pliable.

6. Transfer tortillas to plates and divide 1/8 of the egg mixture down the centre of each one. Roll them up and serve with your favourite garnish.

24. Cinnamon Blueberry Bread

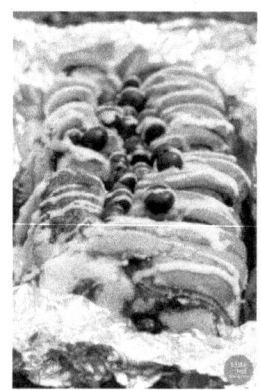

This bread is heavenly with some hot coffee while you marvel at nature all around you. I like to sprinkle some confectioners' sugar on top and serve with fresh fruit.

Preparation Time- 20 minutes
Servings- 8

Ingredients

- 1 loaf of cinnamon bread, sliced
- ½ dozen large eggs
- 4 ounces milk
- 4 ounces heavy cream
- 1 ounce pure maple syrup
- 1 teaspoon vanilla extract
- 16 ounces fresh blueberries, divided
- 8 ounces powdered sugar
- 1 ounce cream

Directions

1. This is best made with hot coals rather than a roaring campfire.

2. Place 2 sheets of thick foil on top of each other and spray with cooking spray. Place bread in the middle of the foil and fold into a bowl with the top of the bread showing. Spread the slices of bread so they are loosely packed.

3. Beat eggs in a bowl with milk, cream, syrup and vanilla.

Pour the egg mixture over the bread, ensuring each slice is saturated in between. Sprinkle half of the blueberries over the bread making sure they get in between each slice.

4. Cover the bread with another sheet of foil and crimp the edges to seal the packet.
5. Place bread on the grate of the fire and cook for 30 minutes until egg is set. Rotate bread to avoid uneven cooking
6. Remove bread from heat and let stand for 10 minutes.

7. Mix 8 ounces of powdered sugar with the cream in a plastic bag and create an icing bag by cutting the corner. Drizzle the top of the bread with the sugar glaze. Serve and enjoy!

25. Camping Quesadillas

I love these breakfast quesadillas with some sour cream, guacamole or ketchup. Who says you can't have dinner for breakfast?

Preparation Time- 20 minutes
Servings - 6
Ingredients

- 8 ounces bulk chicken chorizo sausage
- ½ dozen eggs
- 2 ounces salsa
- 1/8 teaspoon black pepper
- 1/4 teaspoon salt
- 16 ounces Monterey Jack cheese, shredded
- 6 x 12" flour tortillas

Directions
1. Cook sausage in a large frying pan until crumbly and browned evenly.
2. Whisk eggs, 2 ounces of salsa, salt and pepper together in a bowl
3. Cook and stir egg mixture in the pan with the sausage until set and remove to a plate.

4. Clean pan by scraping out excess egg and heat tortillas in the pan

5. Top tortillas with cheese and 1/6 of the egg mixture mixture. Put more cheese on top of the egg, fold the tortilla over and cook for 2 minutes until browned.

6. Flip tortilla over and cook for 1-2 minutes until cheese is melted.

7. Remove from the pan and repeat the process until all quesadillas are cooked.

8. Cut into wedges and serve with your favourite garnishes.

26. Blueberry Orange Muffins

These muffins are fun to make and eat! My kids love throwing the tin foil balls into the fire and will roll their own around and around until it is time to eat.

Preparation Time-15 minutes
Servings-6

- 1 box of blueberry muffin mix and related Ingredients
- 3 oranges, cut in half and hollowed out Make mix according to the instructions on the box

Fill hollowed-out orange halves with muffin batter. Wrap each half with 3 layers of tin foil. Place the tin foil ball in the fire for 10 minutes, turning constantly.
Pull them out, peel and enjoy!

27.Campfire Eclairs

This is another breakfast that can double as a dessert when camping with kids. I love the way these taste and I know the calories will help throughout the morning.

Preparation Time – 15 minutes
Servings – 4

- Tubes of crescent roll dough
- Chocolate pudding
- Whipped cream

Directions
2. Buy some wooden dowels at a craft store and soak them for a few hours before use.
3. Wrap the crescent roll dough around the wet part of the dowel and hold them over the fire until the dough is cooked.
4. Remove crescent roll dough from the dowel and fill with chocolate pudding and top with whipped cream.

28. Toasted Angel Food Cake With Berries

This dessert/breakfast recipe will be a nice sweet treat for any camper after a long night of sleeping under the stars. Don't be scared to toss the tin foil balls in the fire, they won't burn.

Preparation Time-15 minutes
- Angel food cake
- berries

Directions

Place slabs of angel food cake in aluminum foil packets with some berries. Cover with several layers and place in the fire for 10-15 minutes.

Let them stand for a few minutes, uncover and enjoy.

29. Indian Spiced Baked Potato And Egg Foil Packets

This spicy dish is delicious with some hot coffee or tea on a crisp morning. We have this hearty breakfast before we head to the lake for some swimming and fishing.

Preparation Time-15 minutes

- 32 ounces of diced golden yellow potatoes
- 2 ounces olive oil
- 1/2 teaspoon smoked paprika
- 1/2 teaspoon garlic, minced
- 1/2 teaspoon curry powder with turmeric
- 1/4 teaspoon sea salt and
- ¼ teaspoon black pepper
- 4 eggs

Directions
Make a hot campfire.
Toss all Ingredients together in a bowl.

Heat oil in a frying pan and add potatoes. Cook and stir for 20-25 minutes until potatoes are tender inside and crispy outside.

Transfer potatoes to 4 packets of tin foil and crack an egg over the potatoes in each packet. Place on the grate of a fire until eggs are set.

30. Lumberjack Breakfast

Canadians are big campers and the scenery is spectacular when visiting the Provincial Parks in this vast country. This lumberjack breakfast offers the necessary fuel to start a day of exploring.

Preparation Time-20 minutes
Servings-4
Ingredients

- Canadian bacon
- Frozen hash browns
- Eggs
- Chopped tomatoes
- green onions
- Shredded cheddar cheese

Directions:
Place two layers of foil on top of each other and lightly coat with cooking spray
Place bacon on the surface with the cooking spray.

Season with salt and pepper and top with a layer of hash browns, an egg, some diced tomato, green onion and any additional spices.

Seal the tin foil packet and place on the grate of the campfire for 15-20 minutes until meat is cooked. Sprinkle with cheese and cook until it is melted.

Part 2

Introduction

Breakfast is not only the most important meal of the day but it holds great value in achieving weight loss and healthy lifestyle. So in keto diet the importance of this meal increases and it becomes necessary for every keto dieter to incorporate breakfast in the meal plan.

You will be able to learn in this guide about all the health benefits that one can get from breakfast. You will also learn super delicious and healthy recipes to enjoy in your keto breakfast and achieve the weight loss goal quickly.

Life in today's age is quite busy and we hardly find time to get ourselves into the kitchen to prepare something healthy especially breakfast in the morning. If you are one of those who have always been lazy in getting up in the morning and specifying some time to make a healthy breakfast, this book will definitely put some motivation in you to get on the track of healthy living with better understanding of numerous benefits one can get from having breakfast regularly.

You will be able to know in detail about all the nutritional benefits your body gets from the inclusion of keto friendly foods in your breakfast. The recipes are given with preparation info, nutritional breakdown and easy to understand <u>directions</u> that as soon as you go through them, it's all in your mind to prepare the healthy food.

Breakfast And Health Benefits

Breakfast is the most important meal of the day that one cannot afford to skip for healthy mind and body. Your metabolism slows down as you sleep for several hours and it needs to be started again as soon as possible when you get up in the morning in order to supply energy to your brain and other organs of your body.

A healthy breakfast helps you do things with full focus and you are able to perform at your workplace in an efficient way.

Skipping breakfast greatly affects your memory and as a result you lose concentration on your work. So the importance of breakfast cannot be ignored especially in keto diet when you need lots of fats to sustain ketosis in your body and also to meet the energy needs to carry out different activities throughout the day.

Several studies found that the habit of having a regular breakfast is really helpful in reducing the risk of diabetes, heart disease and lowering "bad" LDL cholesterol levels.

The nutrients and vitamins your body gets from the food you have in your breakfast are very important to boost your energy level and help you start your day in an effective way. Many people in today's age don't have a proper breakfast as they are in a hurry to reach their destination as soon as they can.

A breakfast loaded with nutrients gives us many health benefits that you are going to learn in this chapter.

Active body
Today's age is the age of competition and only those people win that stay physically active in their field all the time. You need to keep your body supercharged throughout the day so you don't feel exhausted at all during whatever work you are doing.

A healthy meal early in the morning before you leave your home helps you stay active and energetic throughout the day, and you are more efficient in what you do and can efficiently compete with others. So inclusion of breakfast in your diet is really essential for active and energetic body.

Better eyesight

Eyesight is something which we have to take great care of if we are a professional that spends most of the time before computers screen or at any other workplace where eyesight is likely to be affected.

A breakfast that is enriched with vitamin A greatly helps you improve the health of your eyes and as a result you enjoy powerful eyesight.

So people with weak eyesight should focus on the food containing vitamin A in their breakfast so they not only have better eyesight but also prevent any major eye problems.

Weight loss

It has been proven through research that people who take their breakfast regularly look slim and smart as compared to those who usually skip their morning meal, thinking that they will have a good lunch later in the day.

What happens is that after not having the first important meal of the day, you eat a lot in your lunch time due to feeling very hungry and this ultimately puts you at the risk of being overweight. A Proper breakfast in the morning time helps you keep your appetite in control for the rest of the day and this perfectly fits into the lifestyle of those who are on a weight loss diet.

Control over sugar craving

A great benefit of having breakfast is that it helps us keep control over sugar craving throughout the day.

Every day when we get up in the morning, our body is in need of certain nutrients and it keeps craving food until it receives them. In keto diet sugar craving is something that you have to overcome in any case, you cannot eat anything that contains sugar as an ingredient because your body is in ketosis (a process in which ketones produced by the liver are used as fuel to supply energy to the whole body instead of sugar).

You can eat a keto dessert of your choice in your breakfast if you are one of those people that have a sweet tooth. In keto desserts some specific sweeteners replace sugar, these sweeteners actually make the dessert taste like sugar but they do not cause any increase in the amount of carbs in your body or any other impact to harm the ketosis.

So the crux of the matter is that the very first meal of the day as breakfast definitely helps you control your sugar craving for the rest of the day.

Better brain functioning
Brain is the most important organ in our body, the functionality of which totally depends on what we eat and how we take care of it. People that incorporate breakfast in their diet plan every day not only get better brain functioning but their memory is also very sharp and they excel in their education or job.

From this you can realize how important meal of the day breakfast is for you. Successful people also have a habit of getting a healthy breakfast before they start their day because they know that they will need energy to make their brain function better and achieve all the goals set for that particular day.

Good for diabetes patients
In general breakfast is a meal that is important for everyone for healthy lifestyle but for diabetes people it is the most important. A diabetic person should not skip breakfast in any case as the

sugar level goes low due to keeping stomach empty for several hours.

Going for healthy food options is the best thing for a diabetic person as they really help in maintaining sugar level in the body.

Cardiovascular health

A breakfast that is enriched with dietary fiber definitely helps in controlling cholesterol levels in your body. This is actually good for your cardiovascular health and preventing your heart from any fatal disease.

Incorporation of omega 3 fatty acids and healthy fats in your food strengthens your heart muscles and cells which prevent any stroke or heart attack.

Psychological health improvement

It has been proven through several studies that the consistent breakfast eaters have better psychological health compared to those who often skip this meal. Strong relationship building whether in professional or personal life is really important and it all depends on how strong we psychologically are.

Foods containing minerals like selenium, potassium and magnesium are very effective in boosting the psychological health. Incorporating such foods in your diet helps you properly nourish your brain and protect it from chronic diseases like Alzheimer's disease and Parkinson.

It takes some time to prepare a healthy breakfast so it is very beneficial for you to specify some time each day to make something that is enriched with nutrients and minerals.

Cheese Health Benefits

Cheese is a dairy product that man has been producing in various forms for the purpose of adding value to the overall nutritional intake for thousands of years.

Cheese is enriched with calcium which is very essential for the health of teeth and bones in your body. Calcium also plays a great role in normalizing blood pressure and supporting healing of the wounds.

There is a general perception among many people that dairy products are harmful when you are on the journey of losing weight. This is not true in fact but people would believe it if they are not familiar with the science of keto diet. Cheese can be a part of healthy eating if your body is able to adapt to it especially in keto diet and it also helps you lose weight in order to achieve a healthier and fitter body.

Although there are several types of cheese available in the market but the two main types the cheese has been categorized into are soft cheese and hard cheese.

Soft cheeses like feta and camembert are prepared in a shorter period of time, so that's why they are soft, while on the other hand hard cheeses like cheddar and parmesan take longer time in the production process. There are several popular types of hard cheeses, some take 3 to 6 months and some even require more than a year to be ripened. Mostly the cheddar cheese takes around 6 months while the parmesan cheese need 10 to 24 months depending on what form it is being produced in.

You might be wondering what type of cheese is suitable for you when you are on keto diet. All the types of cheeses are good to be used in keto diet but cheddar cheese is the one that is the best option as it is not only low carb but it is also very enriched with calcium which is the beneficial nutrient for the body. Below are given the important benefits our body can get from cheese.

Healthy Bones

You are on the journey of losing weight and getting fitter and healthier in keto diet but at the same time you cannot ignore the health of your body from several other important aspects.

Incorporation of cheese in your daily food intake helps you prevent many problems related to bones especially osteoporosis. Cheddar and parmesan are the richest dietary sources of calcium which are really helpful in strengthening bones and teeth.

Omega 3 fatty acids

When it comes to omega 3 fatty acids, we find that they are abundantly found in cheese. So this means that making cheese part of your regular diet protects you from the conditions like heart attack, heart valve disease, heart failure, congenital heart disease, coronary artery disease, abnormal heart rhythms, heart muscle disease etc.

It has been proven through research that even if you don't have any disease, the inclusion of appropriate quantity of cheese in your daily diet improves your overall cardiovascular health which ultimately leads to healthy living.

Hunger Control

Having cheese for breakfast leaves a very positive impact on our health in terms of weight loss as it keeps you fuller for longer and you don't overeat at lunch or any other time in the day.

So if you are on keto diet and looking to reduce your weight, then eating cheese in the very first meal of the day is really essential for you.

You have to clearly understand that how much cheese you can eat per day depending on your daily needs. You should know that what ratio of it you can use with other ingredients as eating it in excess might be harmful for your body.

It is obvious that you cannot ignore the calculation of calories you are taking in each meal every single day when you are on a weight loss diet. All you need to do is find out what is your calorie need per day and distribute it among all the meals you will be having every day including breakfast which is of course the crucial meal of the day.

This way you will know exactly what quantity of cheese will be enough for you with other calories in a specific meal, and always remembering that will prevent you from overeating and putting your health at risk. Things will be really easier for you once you are equipped with the knowledge of balancing your calories in a certain recipe knowing that how much you need to add with other ingredients in order to prepare a super delicious and healthy meal.

Some people prefer meal prepping for keto diet so they eat exactly what they need for their body and there is no risk involved in their journey of achieving their weight loss in other health related goals.

It has been observed that sometimes eating too much cheese results in constipation. If you encounter something like that in your keto diet then you can balance things with the help of keto vegetables like zucchini, asparagus, cauliflower, broccoli, etc.

There are some precautions you just have to be bit careful about otherwise cheese is absolutely keto friendly and you can enjoy it in your keto diet making your food super delicious and healthy.

You can choose from a variety of cheeses without any hesitation depending upon what you like as all the types of cheeses are low carb and keto friendly. If you specifically ask a dietitian about any recommendation then most probably the answer you will get is "Cheddar Cheese" as it is enriched with calcium apart from being low carb. Like all the hard cheeses this type of cheese is easy to digest and if you are someone with sensitive stomach then this will be a good option for you.

Something very important for you to remember in the end is that you should always be careful about purchasing this product from the market as brands selling processed cheeses might give you additional fats and salt. So you should always look for the naturally manufactured options.

Butter In Keto Diet And Health Benefits

Butter has been used in food for healthy lifestyle for thousands of years. As most people know that it is actually a dairy product manufactured through the process of churning cream or milk.

Although this amazing and healthy product is prepared from the milk of several animals like buffalos, goats, sheeps etc. but most of the butter available to us in our everyday life is obtained from the cows and that is the reason butter is usually produced in the areas where cows are found in abundance.

Butter is a great source of vitamins and minerals and people love to have it in their breakfast especially with pancakes it generates an amazing taste. When it comes to vitamins, it provides you with vitamin A, D, E and K and the minerals you can get from it are iodine, manganese, zinc, chromium, selenium and copper.

Most of the fats found in butter are very beneficial for our health and really supporting in ketosis.

In the earlier days people had two choices when they went to buy the better, either they had to choose salted or they could go for unsalted. But in today's age another two types of butter that are very important to consider are the grass fed and grain fed butter.

The main difference between these two types is that the grass fed butter is obtained from cows that have access to grass in open pastures while on the other hand grain fed butter is produced from cows that are confined to rooms and are mostly fed with GMO grains.

Let's see how making butter a regular part of our diet benefits our body.

Prevents gastrointestinal problems

A Special kind of fatty acid found in butter called glycosphingolipids protects you from various gastrointestinal problems. What it does is create the resistance against the functioning of bacteria by combining with mucus layers.

Butter contains these fatty acids in huge amount and there is no doubt that making it part of your breakfast regularly keeps your digestive system safe and also goes on strengthening it day by day.

Sexual Health

Apart from Vitamin A, butter is also enriched with Vitamin D and E which are actually fat-soluble and play their role in taking nutrients out of water-soluble vitamins. Studies have found that fat soluble vitamins are effective in improving sexual health.

According to some latest studies, those people have been mostly found to be complaining about their sexual performance that reduced the consumption of butter in their daily diet.

Many people don't know that the best source of fat soluble vitamins is butterfat and its incorporation in their diet can definitely take their sexual health to the next level.

Absorption of nutrients

With so many benefits butter provides to our health, it also contains a special vitamin that is named as "Activator X" that works as a catalyst and helps in the absorption of nutrients in our body.

So the efficiency of our body increases, our energy level goes high with the help of this catalyst and we are able to perform better in different physical activities which might not be possible in its absence as our body cannot absorb those nutrients without that catalyst support.

Thyroid health

Thyroid gland is something most people might know is the backbone of the endocrine system, so from this you can have an idea that how essential it is to take care of its health.

If you are suffering from hypothyroidism or any other thyroid related disease then you are most probably facing the deficiency of vitamin A, which you can easily overcome by including butter in your diet. This powerful nutrient greatly helps in the creation and secretion of hormones throughout the body and makes them function properly.

Protection from Arthritis

Wulzen factor is an important substance found in butter that prevents the joints from calcification, a condition that becomes the cause of Arthritis.

The butter obtained from the milk gone through the process of pasteurization does not contain this substance as it is eliminated in pasteurization. So the naturally produced butter like the grass fed butter is the best choice for the people suffering from Arthritis or any other joints problem.

Improves immune system

Carotene is an important nutrient found in natural butter which helps in the production of antioxidants or vitamin A. Antioxidants are actually very powerful compounds in our body that strengthen the immune system fighting against fatal diseases.

Vitamin A is good for our digestive and urinary tracts as well as for our mouth, throat, eyes and skin. They play a crucial role in the growth of cells and also in repairing the damaged cells.

Vitamin A also boosts the immune system by helping in the production of lymphocytes which are disease fighting cells in our body. It has been proven through several studies that vitamin A are really helpful in creating resistance against AIDS and protecting from respiratory infections.

Nutritional Value Of Eggs In Keto Diet

Eggs hold amazing value from nutritional point of view and one cannot ignore their importance in a breakfast. As we have heard a lot of times in our lives that an apple a day keeps the doctor away, just like that there is a popular saying that an egg a day keeps the doctor away.

Some people are reluctant to make eggs a part of their diet because of their enrichment with cholesterol but the fact is that the cholesterol found in eggs is only harmful for those who are highly sensitive to cholesterol.

Those people who are suffering from any heart disease or encountering any cardiac problem should definitely not include eggs in their diet.

Eggs are one of the most nutritionally enriched foods you can have in your breakfast. An egg contains all the important nutrients that are essential for a healthy body.

You can cook eggs in various forms like boiling, scrambling, poaching or making an omelet when you are in keto diet and you will get amazing nutritional benefits. Let's see how including eggs in keto breakfast can make a difference for a healthy living.

Source of protein

In keto diet our body also needs protein along with fats in certain proportion as it is really important for fitter and healthier body. There are small units in our body called amino acids and these connect together to form long chains which are named as protein.

The importance of protein can be known from the fact that they are involved in the process of building all kinds of tissues in our body and that's the reason they are called the building blocks of life.

Eating one large egg daily provides your body with 6 grams of protein. So this really makes you understand how eating eggs can fulfill the protein needs of your body when you are on keto diet.

Omega - 3 fatty acids

You will definitely be glad to know that you can get lots of omega 3 fatty acids from eggs but one thing important to mention here is that not all eggs provide you with omega 3 fatty acids - these wonderful and highly beneficial nutrients are only available in the eggs obtained from hens that are fed flaxseed and fish oil.

Fish is definitely a good source of omega 3 fatty acids and if somehow you are not able to eat fish then such eggs are an excellent replacement for you to go for.

Boost brain performance

Many people are not aware of the fact that having eggs regularly in diet greatly helps in improving brain health and ultimately our brain starts functioning better.

Brain is actually the most complex organ in our body and in order to keep it in healthy condition, we have to take care of its all nutritional needs. Eggs contain some really powerful vitamins and minerals that provide energy to the brain cells and help in boosting the memory.

Source of good cholesterol

People with heart disease or facing blood pressure problems normally are scared of eating foods containing cholesterol but the important thing here to understand is that the cholesterol is mainly categorized into two types - good cholesterol and bad cholesterol.

High density lipoprotein (HDL) is good cholesterol found in eggs that can help you reduce the risk of heart disease and other heart problems. Our body needs 300 mg of HDL on daily basis and eating two eggs per day easily fulfills this requirement. It has been found in several studies that keeping this habit continuously till 6 months can help us increase the HDL level by 10% in our body.

Healthy Eyes

Eyes are one of the most important organs we are blessed with and without them one cannot imagine to live. Eggs contain an important nutrient called vitamin A, the deficiency of which leads to blindness.

In addition to this, the incorporation of eggs in your daily diet also protects you from the two most common eye disorders "Cataracts" and "Macular" as there are two amazing antioxidants in eggs known as zeaxanthin and lutein. These antioxidants strengthen the retina of our eyes.

RECIPES

Almond Flour Pancakes

Preparation Info:

Prep Time: 5 minutes

Cook Time: 15 minutes

Total Time: 20 minutes

Servings: 4

Nutritional Info:

Fat: 23g | **Protein**: 9g | **Net Carbs**: 4g | **Calories**: 261

Ingredients:

- 2 large eggs
- 2 tbsp avocado oil
- 1 cup almond flour
- 1/3 cup unsweetened almond milk
- 1 tsp gluten-free baking powder
- 1 tsp vanilla extract
- 2 tbsp erythritol
- 1/8 tsp sea salt

Directions:

1. Take a mixing bowl, add eggs, almond flour, baking powder, vanilla extract and mix together all the ingredients until combined.
2. Add almond milk, erythritol, salt to the mixture and keep mixing until smooth batter is ready.
3. Take a pan and preheat it over medium low heat with oil.
4. Pour 1/8 cup of batter in circle form into the preheated pan.
5. Cover the pan and cook for 2 minutes or until you notice bubbles forming at the edges.

6. Flip and cook the other side for 2 minutes or until it gets brown.
7. Remove from the pan once cooked and repeat the process with the remaining batter to cook all the pancakes.
8. Transfer to the serving plate and enjoy the delicious almond flour pancakes.

Blackberry Cobbler

Preparation Info:

Prep Time: 10 minutes

Cook Time: 15 minutes

Total Time: 25 minutes

Servings: 4

Nutritional Info:

Fat: 27g | **Protein**: 7g | **Net Carbs**: 5g | **Calories**: 315

Ingredients:

- 1 egg
- ½ cup almond flour
- 10 oz. fresh blackberries
- 3 oz. butter
- ¼ cup coconut flour
- 2 tbsp lime juice
- 2 tbsp erythritol
- 1 tsp arrowroot powder
- 1 cup heavy whipping cream

Directions:

1. Preheat oven to 350°F and get a pie dish ready for baking.
2. Add the fresh blackberries in the pie dish and squeeze lemon juice at the top.
3. Take the arrowroot powder and sprinkle it all over the blackberries in the pie dish. This actually helps in thickening and mixing well.
4. Take a mixing bowl, add egg, almond flour, coconut flour, whipping cream, erythritol, mix until all the ingredients are well combined and crumbly dough is prepared.
5. Spread the dough over the blackberries in the pie dish.

6. Take the butter, cut into thin slices and spread them at the top of the dough.
7. Place in the preheated oven and bake for 15 minutes or until you notice golden look.
8. Remove from the oven once baked and serve with whipped cream.

Breakfast Brownie Muffins

Preparation Info:

Prep Time: 15 minutes

Cook Time: 15 minutes

Total Time: 30 minutes

Servings: 6

Nutritional Info:

Fat: 14.1g | **Protein**: 7g | **Net Carbs**: 4.4g | **Calories**: 193

Ingredients:

- 1 large egg
- ½ cup pumpkin puree
- 1 cup golden flaxseed meal
- 1 tsp apple cider vinegar
- 1 tbsp cinnamon
- ¼ cup slivered almonds
- ¼ cup cocoa powder
- ¼ cup sugar-free caramel syrup
- ½ tbsp baking powder
- 2 tbsp coconut oil
- 1 tsp vanilla extract
- ½ tsp salt

Directions:

1. Preheat oven to 350°F and get a 3x2 muffin tin ready by lining it with muffin cups.
2. Take a mixing bowl, add golden flaxseed meal, cinnamon, slivered almonds, cocoa powder, baking powder and salt. Mix until all the ingredients are well combined.
3. Take another bowl, add egg, pumpkin puree, apple cider vinegar, caramel syrup, coconut oil and vanilla extract. Mix until well combined.

4. Add the wet ingredients mixture into the dry ingredients mixture and mix until smooth batter is prepared.
5. Specify ¼ cup of batter for each muffin when transferring the batter to the muffin tin.
6. Sprinkle the slivered almonds at the top and press gently.
7. Place in the preheated oven to bake for 15 minutes.
8. Remove from the oven once properly baked and enjoy the delicious breakfast brownie muffins.

Mushroom Ricotta Galette

Preparation Info:

Prep Time: 20 minutes

Cook Time: 25 minutes

Total Time: 45 minutes

Servings: 6

Nutritional Info:

Fat: 33.1g | **Protein**: 21g | **Net Carbs**: 6.9g | **Calories**: 407

Ingredients:

Filling:
- 2 large eggs
- 1/2 cup grated gouda cheese
- 2 1/2 cups brown mushrooms, sliced
- 3/4 cup + 1 tbsp ricotta cheese
- 1 garlic clove, minced
- 3 tbsp butter, divided
- 1 small brown onion, minced
- 2 tbsp fresh thyme
- 1 tbsp extra virgin olive oil

Dough:
- 1 large egg
- 1 1/2 cups shredded mozzarella cheese
- 1 tsp Italian seasoning
- 1 cup almond flour
- 1/2 tsp garlic powder
- 1 tsp onion powder
- 1 heaped tbsp cream cheese

Directions:
1. For the filling, melt half of the butter in a frying pan over medium heat, add mushrooms and keep cooking until brown.
2. Add the remaining butter in a saucepan over medium heat, add onion and garlic when the butter is melted. Cook until you notice softness.
3. Mix eggs, ricotta, thyme leaves and gouda in a bowl until combined. Add the cooked butter mixture and keep stirring until you get a creamy look.
4. For the dough preheat oven to 400°F and microwave cream cheese and mozzarella cheese together in a bowl for 60 seconds, and then for another 30 seconds after stirring to melt.
5. Remove from the oven once melted, stir well, add egg, seasonings and almond flour until soft dough is formed.
6. Spread the dough on a parchment paper and make it thin by putting another parchment paper at the top and rolling out well in circle form.
7. Transfer the filling onto the dough with the help of a spoon leaving some space from the edges and spread mushrooms at the top. Fold and roll out the edges around the filling.
8. Place in the oven to bake for 25 minutes.
9. Remove from the oven once baked properly. Do the olive oil drizzling and garnishing with thyme before you serve the mouth watering mushroom ricotta galette.

Blueberry Pancakes

Preparation Info:

Prep Time: 5 minutes

Cook Time: 20 minutes

Total Time: 25 minutes

Servings: 4

Nutritional Info:

Fat: 44g | **Protein**: 15g | **Net Carbs**: 7g | **Calories**: 478

Ingredients:

- 2/3 cup almond flour
- 3 oz. fresh blueberries
- ½ lemon, the zest
- 4 oz. cream cheese
- 6 eggs
- 2/3 cup oat fiber
- 2 tsp baking powder
- 3 oz. melted butter
- 1 pinch salt

Directions:

1. Add melted butter, eggs and cream cheese in a bowl. Mix together all the ingredients until well blended.
2. Take another mixing bowl, add almond flour, lemon zest, oat fiber, baking powder and salt. Mix until well combined.
3. Pour the almond flour mixture into the butter mixture and keep mixing until smooth batter is prepared.
4. Heat a small non-stick pan over medium heat.
5. Drop 1/3 cup of batter onto the pan in circle form.
6. Cook for 1-2 minutes, add some blueberries gently, flip and cook for 2-3 minutes or until golden brown.

7. Remove from the pan once cooked and repeat the process with the remaining batter to make more pancakes.
8. Transfer the pancakes to the serving plate and serve with whipped cream.

Chocolate Waffles

Preparation Info:

Prep Time: 15 minutes

Cook Time: 20 minutes

Total Time: 35 minutes

Servings: 5

Nutritional Info:

Fat: 26.6g | **Protein**: 7.2g | **Net Carbs**: 1.9g | **Calories**: 289

Ingredients:

- 3 tbsp full fat milk
- 25 g cocoa unsweetened
- 2 tsp vanilla
- 5 eggs
- 110 g butter, melted
- 4 tbsp granulated swerve
- 4 tbsp coconut flour
- 1 tsp baking powder

Directions:

1. Crack the eggs and separate the whites and yolks in two different bowls.
2. Take the egg whites and whisk until you achieve the firmness and notice stiff peaks forming.
3. Take another bowl, add coconut flour, baking powder, cocoa, granulated swerve and egg yolks. Mix until all the ingredients are well combined.
4. Add the melted butter to the mixture while mixing at the same time to make sure you maintain the smoothness.
5. Add full fat milk and vanilla to the mixture and mix until well combined.

6. Take the whisked egg whites and add to the flour mixture slowly with the help of spoons while ensuring the fluffiness in the mixture.
7. Fill the waffle maker with the mixture and cook for 20 minutes or until you get a golden brown look.
8. Repeat the process with the remaining mixture to cook the waffles.
9. Transfer to the serving plate and enjoy the amazing chocolate waffles.

Creamy Keto Oatmeal

Preparation Info:

Prep Time: 10 minutes

Cook Time: 20 minutes

Total Time: 30 minutes

Servings: 2

Nutritional Info:

Fat: 58.1g | **Protein**: 15.7g | **Net Carbs**: 14.7g | **Calories**: 659

Ingredients:

- 1/4 cup flax seed
- 1 cup blueberry
- 1 2/3 cup almond milk
- 1/2 cup almonds
- 8-10 stevia drops
- 2 tbsp shredded coconut
- 1/2 cup macadamia nuts
- 1 pinch salt
- Cinnamon
- Vanilla extract

Directions:

1. Grind macadamia nuts, flaxseeds and almonds one by one in a food processor. Make sure that each ingredient is finely ground.
2. Take a saucepan and tip the flaxseeds and nuts in that, and then add almond milk, shredded coconut, vanilla extract, stevia and salt.
3. Stir well to combine all the ingredients in the saucepan and cook for 10 minutes or until thick.
4. Put another saucepan over medium heat, add few tablespoons of water in that and place the blueberries in it.

5. Keep cooking until the blueberries are broken down into a jell form.
6. Remove from the heat once ready, transfer the oatmeal into serving bowl.
7. Top with blueberry jam, sprinkle with cinnamon and enjoy the delicious creamy keto oatmeal.

Rosemary Keto Bagels

Preparation Info:

Prep Time: 10 minutes

Cook Time: 45 minutes

Total Time: 55 minutes

Servings: 4

Nutritional Info:

Fat: 22.5g | **Protein**: 13g | **Net Carbs**: 4.5g | **Calories**: 285

Ingredients:

- 1 whole egg
- 3/4 teaspoon xanthan gum
- 1/2 cup warm water
- 3/4 tsp baking soda
- 1 tbsp rosemary, chopped
- 3 egg whites
- 1 1/2 cups almond flour
- 3 tbsp psyllium husk powder
- 1/4 tsp salt
- Avocado oil for coating

Directions:

1. Preheat oven to 250°F and get the bagel mold ready by coating it with avocado oil.
2. Take a mixing bowl, add almond flour, baking soda, xanthan gum and salt. Mix together all the ingredients until well combined.
3. Crack the eggs in another bowl, whisk well, add the warm water and mix until combined.
4. Add the liquid mixture to the dry mixture, mix until fully combined and the dough is ready.

5. Transfer the dough to the bagel mold and sprinkle rosemary at the top.
6. Place in the oven to bake for 45 minutes or until properly baked.
7. Remove from the oven once baked and allow to cool for few minutes.
8. Make the slices, transfer to the serving plate and enjoy the lovely rosemary keto bagels.

Mexican Breakfast Hash

Preparation Info:

Prep Time: 5 minutes

Cook Time: 20 minutes

Total Time: 25 minutes

Servings: 2

Nutritional Info:

Fat: 34.9g | **Protein**: 22.8g | **Net Carbs**: 7.5g | **Calories**: 452

Ingredients:

- 1/2 cup chopped tomatoes
- 2 large eggs
- 1 tbsp ghee
- 1/2 cup diced avocado
- 1/2 cup sliced green pepper
- 2 cups chopped chard
- 1/2 small white onion, chopped
- 6 oz Mexican chorizo, casing removed
- 1 cup chopped zucchini
- Fresh cilantro for garnish
- Salt and pepper to taste

Directions:

1. Put a skillet over medium high heat after greasing it with ghee. Add chopped onion, cook for a minute, then add sliced green pepper and cook for another 3 minutes while stirring.
2. Add chopped tomatoes and diced zucchini and cook for 4 minutes uncovered while stirring with small intervals.
3. Add the Mexican chorizo and cook for 4-5 minutes.
4. Add the chopped chard and cook for 3 minutes more.

5. Make two wells in the cooked mixture with the help of a spatula and crack the eggs in them.
6. Transfer to the broiler after adding salt and pepper.
7. Cook under the broiler on high for 4-5 minutes or until egg whites are set but egg yolks are still juicy.
8. Remove from the broiler once cooked, transfer to the serving plate.
9. Top with diced avocado, garnish with cilantro and enjoy the delicious Mexican breakfast hash.

Cauliflower Hash Browns

Preparation Info:

Prep Time: 10 minutes

Cook Time: 40 minutes

Total Time: 50 minutes

Servings: 4

Nutritional Info:

Fat: 26g | **Protein**: 7g | **Net Carbs**: 5g | **Calories**: 278

Ingredients:

- 3 eggs
- 4 oz. butter
- 15 oz. cauliflower
- ½ yellow onion, grated
- 2 pinches pepper
- 1 tsp salt

Directions:

1. Get the cauliflower ready by rinsing, trimming and grating with the help of food processor.
2. Take a large bowl, add the grated cauliflower, eggs, onion, salt and pepper. Mix together all the ingredients and set aside for few minutes.
3. Put a large skillet over medium heat and melt butter in that.
4. Take scoops of the cauliflower mixture, place in the skillet and flatten them using spatula making sure that their size reaches to 3-4 inches.
5. Cook one side for 4-5 minutes or until brown, then flip and cook the other side for 4-5 minutes. Be careful while flipping.
6. Remove from the skillet once properly cooked, transfer to the serving plate and enjoy the amazing cauliflower hash browns.

Berries Cream Cake

Preparation Info:

Prep Time: 5 minutes

Cook Time: 4 minutes

Total Time: 9 minutes

Servings: 1

Nutritional Info:

Fat: 65g | **Protein**: 16g | **Net Carbs**: 8g | **Calories**: 671

Ingredients:

- 1/4 cup mixed berries
- 1/4 cup almond flour
- 2 large eggs
- 2 tbsp ghee
- 2 tbsp cream cheese (RT)
- 1/4 cup sugar free vanilla syrup
- 1/2 tbsp sugar free brown sugar syrup
- 1/4 cup whipping cream

Directions:

1. Melt ghee in a pan over medium heat and set aside to cool.
2. Pour the melted ghee in a bowl when cool.
3. Add vanilla syrup, eggs and cream cheese to the bowl and mix together all the ingredients using hand mixer until smooth.
4. Transfer the mixture to a mug and stir in the almond flour.
5. Stir in the mixed berries to the mixture and microwave for 3-4 minutes.
6. Blend brown sugar syrup and whipping cream in another bowl until you notice the stiffness.
7. Top with whipped cream and enjoy the yummy berries cream cake.

Classic French Omelet

Preparation Info:

Prep Time: 20 minutes

Cook Time: 5 minutes

Total Time: 25 minutes

Servings: 1

Nutritional Info:

Fat: 41g | **Protein**: 22g | **Net Carbs**: 2g | **Calories**: 470

Ingredients:

- 1.5 tbsp butter (chilled and cubed)
- 1 tbsp heavy whipping cream
- 3 large eggs
- 1/4 tsp black pepper
- 1 large yolk
- 1 tbsp fresh parsley
- 1/2 tsp pink Himalayan salt

Directions:

1. Take a mixing bowl, add heavy whipping cream, yolk, eggs, parsley, salt and pepper. Mix until you get a frothy look and set the mixture aside for few minutes to sit properly.
2. Take 1tbsp of chilled and cubed butter and add to the egg mixture.
3. Put a non-stick skillet over low heat and add the remaining butter into it.
4. Pour the egg mixture into the skillet once the butter is fully melted.
5. Use the spatula to spread over the surface of skillet and scrap from the sides. Cook the mixture for 5 minutes or until firmed.

6. Remove from the heat once the eggs are firmed and cover with lid for 2 minutes.
7. Roll into an omelet with the help of spatula.
8. Transfer to the serving plate and enjoy the delicious classic French omelet.

Cheesy Waffles

Preparation Info:

Prep Time: 10 minutes

Cook Time: 2 minutes

Total Time: 12 minutes

Servings: 4

Nutritional Info:

Fat: 16.9g | **Protein**: 13.4g | **Net Carbs**: 2.1g | **Calories**: 215

Ingredients:

- 1/2 cup grated cheddar cheese
- 1 tsp mixed dried Italian herbs
- 3 large eggs
- 1/2 tsp gluten-free baking powder
- 1/4 cup cream cheese (RT)
- 1/2 tsp garlic powder
- 1/2 tsp onion powder
- 1/3 cup grated parmesan cheese
- 1 tbsp coconut flour
- 3 tbsp flax meal
- Salt and pepper to taste

Directions:

1. Preheat the waffle maker while you are getting the batter ready.
2. Crack the eggs into a mixing bowl, add the cream cheese and mix until smooth.
3. Add grated parmesan cheese, cheddar cheese to the egg mixture and mix until well combined.
4. Take another bowl, add coconut flour, baking powder, flaxmeal, garlic powder, mixed dried Italian herbs, onion

powder, salt and pepper. Mix together all the ingredients.

5. Add the dry ingredients mixture into the wet ingredients mixture and keep mixing until a smooth batter is prepared.
6. **Transfer** the batter to the waffle maker and cook for 2 minutes or until properly done.
7. Move to the serving plate and enjoy the mouth watering cheesy waffles.

Rutabaga Avocado Fritters

Preparation Info:

Prep Time: 10 minutes

Cook Time: 20 minutes

Total Time: 30 minutes

Servings: 4

Nutritional Info:

Fat: 113g | **Protein**: 25g | **Net Carbs**: 14g | **Calories**: 1211

Ingredients:

Rutabaga fritters:
- 4 eggs
- 1/8 tsp turmeric
- 15 oz. rutabaga
- ¼ tsp pepper
- 8 oz. halloumi cheese
- 4 oz. butter
- 3 tbsp coconut flour
- 1 tsp salt

Ranch mayonnaise:
- 1 tbsp ranch seasoning
- 1 cup mayonnaise

For serving:
- 5 1/3 oz. leafy greens
- 4 avocados

Directions:

1. Preheat oven to 250°F to keep the patties warm while you are cooking the remaining patties.
2. Grate the rutabaga coarsely after rinsing and peeling.
3. Grate the cheese and take a large bowl, add the grated cheese, grated rutabaga, eggs, turmeric, coconut flour, salt, pepper and set aside the batter for few minutes to sit properly.
4. Prepare 12 patties from the batter and melt butter in a frying pan over medium high heat.
5. Make two batches of 6 patties, put the first batch into the frying pan.
6. Cook one side for 4-5 minutes or until golden brown.
7. Flip and cook the other side for 4-5 minutes.
8. Repeat the process with the second batch of patties.
9. Transfer the cooked fritters to serving plate and enjoy with sliced avocado, salad and mayonnaise.

French Toast Muffins

Preparation Info:

Prep Time: 10 minutes

Cook Time: 25 minutes

Total Time: 35 minutes

Servings: 11

Nutritional Info:

Fat: 28.1 | **Protein**: 37.6g | **Net Carbs**: 2.1g | **Calories**: 429

Ingredients:

- 1/4 cup heavy cream
- 1 tbsp unsalted butter
- 6 eggs
- 1 tsp cinnamon
- 2/3 cup almond flour
- 1/4 tsp nutmeg
- 1/4 cup peanut butter
- 10 drops stevia
- 2 tbsp erythritol
- 2 tbsp coconut oil
- 1/4 cup toasted almonds
- 1/2 tsp salt
- 1 tsp vanilla extract

Directions:

1. Preheat oven to 350°F and get the cupcake tray ready for baking.
2. Take ¼ cups of almonds and grind them into small pieces in a food processor.
3. Toast the ground almonds in a pan over medium high heat. Keep stirring while almonds are being toasted.

4. Take a large mixing bowl, add almond flour, cinnamon, nutmeg, erythritol and salt. Mix together all the ingredients.
5. Add butter, coconut oil and peanut butter in a microwave bowl and microwave for half a minute or until all the ingredients are melted.
6. Pour the melted ingredients into a large mixing bowl. Add eggs, stevia and vanilla extract and mix well.
7. Add the almond flour mixture, heavy cream and mix until thin batter is prepared.
8. Transfer the batter into the cupcake tray holes.
9. Spread the ground roasted almonds at the top.
10. Place the tray in the oven to bake for 25 minutes or until properly baked.
11. Remove from the oven once baked, allow to cool for few minutes, and then transfer to wire rack to cool completely.
12. Transfer to the serving platter, top with whipped cream and enjoy the delicious French toast muffins.

Conclusion

Keto diet is one of the best ways to lose weight and live a healthy lifestyle. All you need is a proper guideline and right directions while following this diet to get the best results.

I have rendered every possible effort to make this book a powerful tool for you to achieve your weight loss and other health related goals. I would really appreciate if you spare few minutes of your precious time and post an honest review on Amazon. Your feedback as a reader will let me know what you think and how I can bring more helpful books on keto diet for you.

Thanks and all the best for your endeavors!

www.ingramcontent.com/pod-product-compliance
Lightning Source LLC
Chambersburg PA
CBHW071439070526
44578CB00001B/144